Meditations of the Heart

A Prayer Devotional

By Joanne L. Gunning

Editor: Leslie Santamaria
Orlando, Florida

Printing and Book Design: Arthur Printing
Cape Coral, Florida

First Edition, 2000
Printed in the United States of America

Meditations of the Heart:
A Prayer Devotional

© Copyright 2000 Joanne L. Gunning
All rights reserved. Contents may not be reproduced without written permission from the copyright holder, Joanne L. Gunning

Ultimate design, content, and editorial accuracy of this work is the responsibility of the author.

Scripture taken from the HOLY BIBLE, NEW INTERNATIONAL VERSION®. NIV®. Copyright © 1973, 1978, 1984 by International Bible Society. Used by permission of Zondervan Publishing House.

ISBN 0-9701457-0-5
Library of Congress Control Number: 00-191049

Dedicated to Sons

Michael K. and Timothy S. Gunning

Michael and Timothy, you have given me great joy in my journey. You have been my inspiration to pen *Meditations of the Heart.*

"We live by faith, not by sight."
2 Corinthians 5:7

Acknowledgement

A very special thank you to my devoted husband who has consistently demonstrated, through application, the meaning of perseverance. Following your example, I am learning how to take risks … to step out. Thank you, my friend, for encouraging me to chase my dream and to pen these words for our children and our children's children and for all who desire to mine God's Word for treasure.

God burdens hearts to pray. Without prayer this book would not have been published. Thank You, Lord, for every heartfelt prayer breathed on my behalf.

"Let us not become weary in doing good, for at the proper time we will reap a harvest if we do not give up."
Galatians 6:9

Preface

It is in suffering that we begin to understand our character weaknesses and to look beyond ourselves for answers. *Meditations of the Heart* is a prayer devotional comprising 365 daily meditations which offer "kernels of faith"—the central part of faith—found only in Jesus Christ. We are precious seed crushed in His hand, for His purposes.

My prayer is that you will be encouraged to draw nearer to God. He is a Friend that extends an invitation to all: "Give ear and come to me; hear me, that your soul may live" (Isa. 55:3a).

Come and drink from the Fountain of Living Water. He will quench your thirst.

January 1

God is Sovereign

"O Sovereign Lord, you are God! Your words are trustworthy, and you have promised these good things to your servant." (2 Sam. 7:28)

We can't see the road ahead, which is intermingled with straightaways, detours, curves, and blind spots. Prayer is our compass. We know that You will place guideposts along our journey's path to guide and instruct us in the way we should go. When paths become obstructed with sin, show us the error of our ways and redirect our steps. O Lord, help us to remain faithful. Amen.

MEDITATION:
Because God is Sovereign, all things are possible.

> Pour out your longings; He is listening.
> Come face to face with untold heartaches.
> Taste the faithful waters of His Sovereignty;
> Drink in the love that only God can quench!

ss ≥s

January 2

O Blessed Trinity

"For God did not call us to be impure, but to live a holy life." (1 Thess. 4:7)

God, help us to fully rely on Your grace for every step of our spiritual journey. Richly tasting Your Word, may we be devoted to prayer (Col.4:2) for our daily nourishment. Stir in our hearts the desire to grow and to climb new spiritual heights. Hold our hands, Abba, Father, and lead us along divinely appointed paths. Melt all fear as we soar on wings of faith! Amen.

MEDITATION:
O Blessed Trinity! Father, Son, and Holy Spirit—three persons in one.

O Blessed Trinity!
Power from on high…
Fill imperfect hearts;
Come dwell in me.

O Blessed Trinity!
Blow upon my face…
Revive me with Your grace;
Come dwell in me.

January 3

Trust is Learned

"And we rejoice in the hope of the glory of God. Not only so, but we also rejoice in our sufferings, because we know that suffering produces perseverance; perseverance, character; and character, hope. And hope does not disappoint us, because God has poured out his love into our hearts by the Holy Spirit, whom he has given us." (Rom. 5:2b–5)

Father, because of Christ's obedience, we are the righteousness of Christ. We have been redeemed. We are not our own. Shape our lives; work in us. Help us to become the person You see in us. May our trials bear fruit; may our character develop into the very nature of Christ, knowing that our faith has a chance to grow and to develop when we are tested. Help us not to resist the presence of Your Spirit nor wisdom from above. Amen.

MEDITATION:

Trust is learned in the school of faith.

Courage means facing fear;
Mastery is proficient skill.
Armed and ready to move upward,
We are mobilized with God's will.

January 4

Mercy and Love

"There will always be poor people in the land. Therefore I command you to be openhanded toward your brothers and toward the poor and needy in your land." (Deut. 15:11)

Father, direct our hearts to generously give to others. May we be slow to judge and quick to seek Your face. May mercy and kindness rule over us like a sweet and precious fragrance, flowing outward, touching and pointing others to You. Amen.

Meditation:
If I have not experienced the burdens my brothers and sisters bear, then let me bear the mercy and love of Christ.

> Hearts open wide,
> Filling the earth…
> Emptying treasure.

෴

January 5

Our Defense and Shield

"Defend the cause of the weak and fatherless; maintain the rights of the poor and oppressed. Rescue the weak and needy; deliver them from the hand of the wicked." (Ps. 82:3–4)

Father, powerfully You work through us to accomplish Your mighty acts of mercy and justice. May we willingly count the cost and esteem the privilege, knowing that following You, Lord, is life lived to the fullest measure. Father, order our steps and establish our hands to achieve Your purposes. Do not let our hearts shrink from those "hard places" where valuable lessons are learned. Show us that humble beginnings are not to be despised, but to be valued for their precious treasures unearthed. Amen.

MEDITATION:
God is our defense and shield.

> Enemies on every side,
> Feasting on human misery.
> Temptation's prowler,
> Eager to devour
> Unsuspecting hearts.
> Stand strong; be children of valor…
> His spirit draws us near…
> We need not fear.

January 6

His Path of Peace and Goodwill

"All the ways of the Lord are loving and faithful for those who keep the demands of his covenant." (Ps. 25:10)

Lord, the fragrance and beauty of obedience are the gifts of peace and goodwill. You have a plan for each one of us. May we eagerly desire all that you have planned. Every assignment originates from Your own divine plan and is anointed with love and marked with purpose. You are the Truth; the only true God on earth and in heaven. Help us to inquire to You, Lord, for direction and wisdom. You are worthy of reverence and honor and trust. Teach us to reach out to You, Lord, in childlike faith and dependence. You are a good and faithful Father. Answer our prayers according to Your will, and not according to our misunderstandings. Amen.

MEDITATION:
As we draw nearer to Jesus, His path of peace and goodwill become an open channel invigorated with His sweet anointed fragrance.

He presses in on every side,
Tenderly pursuing His Bride.
Rejoice! Rejoice! O heart of mine;
Christ, the Groom, is walking by.

January 7

You Are My Security

"'If I have put my trust in gold or said to pure gold, "You are my security," if I have rejoiced over my great wealth, the fortune my hands had gained, if I have regarded the sun in its radiance or the moon moving in splendor, so that my heart was secretly enticed and my hand offered them a kiss of homage, then these also would be sins to be judged, for I would have been unfaithful to God on high.'"
(Job 31:24–28)

Security is found in You, Lord. The earth is Yours and all that is in it. Father, help me to be an excellent steward of Your goods and finances and talents. Let my first fruits be a reminder that everything I have comes from Your hand. Teach me, Lord, to look to You for my daily bread. Let my heart be aware of Your constant care for me. Remind me that Your thoughts are always toward me. Give me a generous spirit to serve You. When I fall short of the mark, show me my transgressions. Forgive my sins. Strengthened by Your might, I cast down all "things" that clamor for a place in my heart, and I open my heart for You to fill. Amen.

MEDITATION:
You are my security.

God's love is without strings.
False security is fleeting…
Gold mounted up on wings!

January 8

Christ Enables

"She watches over the affairs of her household and does not eat the bread of idleness." (Prov. 31:27)

Faithfully You meet all of our needs through distribution of gifts, talents, and skills. Help us to develop our God-given creativity and uniqueness. Help us to not languish in the temptation of despair, or gossip, or laziness, or fear. Teach us how to tenderly touch others with Your love in thought, word, and deed. May the seeds of kindness be planted and begin to multiply in our lives. May we be dispensers of Your blessings. Amen.

MEDITATION:
Christ enables us to succeed.

> Bread of Life,
> Where fullness dwells,
> Offers hungry souls Himself.
> An invitation to come and taste
> Fulfillment and eternal grace.

January 9

His Hands

"They were all trying to frighten us, thinking, 'Their hands will get too weak for the work, and it will not be completed.' But I prayed, 'Now strengthen my hands.'" (Neh. 6:9)

Belief in and total reliance upon God provides us with peace of mind and spiritual might. We stand back and patiently watch for the glory of God to move. We receive revelation knowledge and wondrous insights as we think upon the things of God. We have the mind of Christ and seek to know His perceptions about our problems or burdens. His Word is our sustenance. His Word is the Voice we seek. O Holy Spirit, there are moments when a situation arises and we can only utter a few words. You take those utterances before our

Father and intercede through us. Thank You for Your indescribable fellowship. Amen.

MEDITATION:
His hands formed my hands.

> He moves
> With purpose…
> We are stretched.
> Esteemed by God…
> We seek His pleasure.
> He establishes our way.

~ ~

January 10
A Gift from God

"For the sake of Jacob my servant, of Israel my chosen, I summon you by name and bestow on you a title of honor, though you do not acknowledge me." (Isa. 45:4)

You have recorded my name, Lord. Your great love has redeemed me. My identification is in You. Your Spirit is housed inside. It's too wondrous to comprehend! Your grace is sufficient. And when my life on earth has passed away, and the tent pegs are removed, I'll be in Your presence, my eternal dwelling place, face to face with perpetual Glory. What a wonderful God we serve. Amen.

MEDITATION:
His "title of honor" isn't earned. It is a gift from God who has no favorites.

> He remains on our journey,
> Giving our lives purpose,
> Expanding our minds,
> Enlarging our hearts.
> Lord, teach us how to serve,
> Forgetting benefits and gratification,
> As we remember Your sacrificial love.

~ ~

January 11

The Fulfilled Desires of the Lord

"He has showed you, O man, what is good. And what does the Lord require of you? To act justly and to love mercy and to walk humbly with your God." (Micah 6:8)

Dear Lord, You cannot be appeased or bought with money or possessions. The whole earth is Yours! Foolish man. Redemption and forgiveness are only found in You. Your shed blood cleanses and removes sin's ugly stain. What do You ask of us? To turn from our sinful ways. Obedience is love in action. Love is serving You. When we seek Your heart's desires, all else will be added. Amen.

MEDITATION:

All that really matters is that we choose to live for Christ. When His desires become our desires, we experience abundant living in Christ.

>   Abundant living is
>   Traveling with God
>   Along uncharted courses,
>   Taking along faith,
>   A seal of promise,
>   His eternal endorsement.

January 12

Firm Steps

"If the Lord delights in a man's way, he makes his steps firm; though he stumble, he will not fall, for the Lord upholds him with his hand." (Ps. 37:23–24)

Father, I am steadied by Your hand. Help me to stay focused. Grant me direction, guidance, wisdom, counsel, and encouragement.

When I stumble, You promise to catch me from falling. I am comforted knowing Your eye is upon me. You watch my every move. You are with me. Moment by moment, You are with me. Even when my hand reaches out in darkness, Your light shines forth hope. Thank You for Your faithfulness and constancy. Amen.

MEDITATION:
Firm steps on a firm foundation.

> No firmer foundation
> Than our Lord…
> O Rock of strength,
> O gentle Spirit.
> Though we run ahead
> And make wrong choices,
> You bring counsel, comfort, and cheer.
> When growing is painful,
> Lessons hurtful,
> We hold on to Truth that is pure!

January 13

Growing Seasons

"As they pass through the Valley of Baca, they make it a place of springs; the autumn rains also cover it with pools. They go from strength to strength, till each appears before God in Zion."
(Ps. 84:6–7)

Your Word brings us hope and comfort, as we pass through our valley of weeping. Your Holy Spirit bursts forth from inside us to create springs—pools of refreshment. You send autumn rains into our dry, parched seasons. Each lesson, each experience builds strength of character. We are strong for battle. We can face conflict and endure pain as we remember and recount Your faithfulness. We are purified in the Refiner's fire. You are with us. Lead us through the storms, and display the rainbow of promise. Amen.

MEDITATION:
　　We are strengthened in the growing seasons.

>　　　During the dry season,
>　　　We thirst.
>　　　Upward we look,
>　　　God's face we seek.
>　　　New beginnings,
>　　　Second chances.
>　　　Leaving outgrown nests,
>　　　We face our fears, and
>　　　God bears us on His wings.

January 14

The Goodness of God

"Taste and see that the Lord is good; blessed is the man who takes refuge in him." (Ps. 34:8)

　　Father, I have tasted Your goodness; Your word brings health to my soul. My hope is in You. I love You, Lord. Forgive my sins and those I've sinned against. Speak to me, Lord, and lead me into Your everlasting way. To *know* that You have my best interests at heart keeps my heart kindled with hopeful expectation. In weakness, quicken me with strength. In forgetfulness, awaken me with the remembrance of Your faithfulness. Amen.

MEDITATION:
　　Nothing compares to the goodness of God.

>　　　Riches don't satisfy…
>　　　The fire grows dim…
>　　　The goodness of God
>　　　Ignites hope again.

January 15

God's Custody

"The Lord will keep you from all harm—he will watch over your life; the Lord will watch over your coming and going both now and forevermore." (Ps. 121:7–8)

Our lives are in Your hands. You are Sovereign. You are Wisdom. We surrender the things we don't understand. Tenderly You prune, cropping off those things that displease You, that bind and interfere with spiritual growth. Faithfully You water; faithfully You wait. Take pleasure, my Lord, in what You have created. Amen.

MEDITATION:
The best possible place to be is in God's custody.

> Tests will come,
> Doubts and peril;
> Light grows dim;
> Darkness invades.
> We walk by faith and not by sight,
> Clinging to God with all our might…
> God's strength prevails.

৵ ৽

January 16

Diligence

"Blessed are all who fear the Lord, who walk in his ways. You will eat the fruit of your labor; blessings and prosperity will be yours." (Ps. 128:1–2)

O God, You are loving and gracious, compassionate and merciful. Place a hedge around us that we might not roam. When we are tempted to shrink back, forgive us. Forgive us Lord, when temptation overcomes us. Help us to be diligent. Quicken our hearts to press on. Your glorious messengers encircle and encourage us. Give us spiritual insights and discerning spirits as we face and accept those boundaries that we cannot cross, boundaries that are created as built-in safeguards. Open our ears to hear, and prepare our hearts to receive. Amen.

Meditation:
Diligence determines quantity and quality of fruit.

> Keep on going,
> Though the way appears dim.
> Press on…Lean in…
> Put your trust in Him.
> Keep reaching out
> To heights unknown;
> Our King reigns
> And is in control!

January 17

God Speaks Peace

"The Lord your God is with you, he is mighty to save. He will take great delight in you, he will quiet you with his love, he will rejoice over you with singing." (Zeph. 3:17)

Your love is the perfect antidote in hard times and in good times, in mountaintop experiences and in dark valleys, in sickness and in health. Your love, Father, soothes our trembling hearts. The cares of this world melt as You gently, oh so softly, quiet our pounding hearts. Singing echoes from Your throne. A lullaby is sung. Softly and tenderly You rejoice over Your children. Amen.

MEDITATION:
God speaks peace in the eye of the storm.

> Rejoicing hearts sing,
> In perfect harmony,
> Praises to the King.

Storms roll in;
Songs grow dim;
Fear rears its head again.

Fear not! Trust God!
Our cries are heard;
Our Lord is in the storm.

Softly He sings,
Quieting hearts
With a lullaby of love.

※ ※

January 18

A Right Heart Attitude

"Be sure to keep the commands of the Lord your God and the stipulations and decrees he has given you." (Deut. 6:17)

We are needy. Lord, we need to do what You ask us to do. We need to go where You send us. We need to listen…You are speaking. We need to see with spiritual eyes and to honestly perceive what You display before our eyes, as if we are looking through Your eyes. As Your love touches us, we need to touch others. As Your mercy is extended toward us, we need to give mercy to others. We need to share the burdens of others and feel what they feel. Yes, we need to be active and courageous and to touch Your earth with the Good News of hope and spiritual rebirth. Amen.

MEDITATION:
A right heart attitude discovers joy in the journey.

Attitude colors a world with rainbows
Or drapes dark puffy clouds in the skies…
Perceiving God's best interest in us
Brightens thoughts in our minds.

※ ※

January 19

The Greatest Star

"'From the heavens the stars fought, from their courses they fought against Sisera…March on, my soul; be strong!'" (Judges 5:20–21b)

Lord, nothing can thwart Your plan. When we are obedient to faithfully answer Your call and to follow Your directives, we cannot fail. We are moving and going forth in Your supernatural strength. Heaven will move on our behalf to accomplish Your purposes. Thank You, Jesus, for truth that shapes our minds. Because of Your grace and great mercy, we can overcome evil with good. Amen.

MEDITATION:
The greatest star wins the battle: Jesus Christ, our Morning Star.

> Who is mighty in battle?
> Who is swift with the Sword?
> Fighting forces of darkness
> With the Light of His Word,
> Secret weapons are wielded
> In the hands of our Lord.

January 20

Communication with God

"[He] stilled the roaring of the seas, the roaring of their waves, and the turmoil of the nations." (Ps. 65:7)

Father, thank you for the quiet. Help me to refocus my thoughts on the majesty and trustworthiness of Your Name. I'm refreshed as Your Spirit touches my body, bringing serenity to my mind, my heart, and my emotions. Ceasing to struggle, tensions subside and peace comes. Amen.

MEDITATION:
Daily communication with God is a great connection.

> God brings calm to the roaring din
> As we seek a place to meet with Him.
> When answers are slow to come,
> We remain steadfast in God's love.

◆◇◆

January 21

Enjoy What Has Been Given to You

"Who has a claim against me that I must pay? Everything under heaven belongs to me." (Job 41:11)

Dear Lord, oftentimes we reflect on those things that we feel we deserve. Our attitudes grow sour as our impatience grows. Stir in our hearts the gift of atonement, freeing us from eternal separation from You. Forgive us when we forget the costliest Gift. Forgive us for grieving Your heart. May we give homage to our Giver of life, and not the gifts—now and forevermore. Amen.

MEDITATION:
Be content with what has already been given.

> Have we sifted through our hands
> The love and mercy of our Lord,
> Failing to appreciate
> The greatest love to contemplate?
> Are we eager to ignore,
> In contempt have we deplored,
> His bountiful gifts to us?
>
> God's Sacrifice, Jesus, paid the price
> With His very life
> To give to us a better place,
> Our eternal home through heaven's gates.

We had no way to purchase or behold
A mansion created by our Lord,
Without our Savior's grace.

❦

January 22

Daily Communion

"I meditate on your precepts and consider your ways." (Ps. 119:15)

Your Word brings health to my bones and renewed strength to my frame. The very taste of Your Word is medicine to my soul, freeing my mind, untangling the confusion wrapped around my thoughts. You are my hope. Keep my soul healthy as I walk in the freedom of Your wisdom and grace. Help me to only glance back as a means to understand—not as a measure of success or failure. Amen.

MEDITATION:
Daily communion with Christ protects us from spiritual malaise.

> Prayer and meditation…
> Soul medicine…restfulness…
> God's counsel so sweet.
> Appointed times…seasons…
> Discovery… secret treasure…
> Waiting to be released.
> Spiritual muscles stretched…
> Questions…answers…more questions…
> Truth…denial…more truth…
> God's Word changes me.

❦

January 23

Carry Your Cross and Follow Me

"Turn my heart toward your statutes and not toward selfish gain."
(Ps. 119:36)

We often give in to the carnal ways of survival in this sin-torn world. To resist the Holy Spirit's control in our lives brings bitter disappointment and pain. Productive years are bargained for empty and barren years. Help us to give "self" back to you, under the leadership of the Holy Spirit. Amen.

MEDITATION:
The right direction is God's direction.

> Life bears a heavy cross…
> Eternal lessons always cost.
> Out of evil good can come…
> Jesus Christ has already won!

January 24

Partnership in Christ

"I urge You, brothers, by our Lord Jesus Christ and by the love of the Spirit, to join me in my struggle by praying to God for me."
(Rom. 15:30)

Thank You for prayer, Father. Through Jesus Christ and the love of the Spirit (a fruit of the Spirit), we can join our brothers and sisters in their struggles. Distance, time, circumstances, obstacles, and emotions cannot prevent us from kneeling before our Lord and interceding for others. "Five of you will chase a hundred, and a hundred of you will chase ten thousand" (Lev. 26:8a). What power in the name of Jesus. Keep us in Your perfect will, Father. May sin not rule over us. Sin is not welcome in our bodies, which is the temple of the living God. May our prayers be unhindered by living pure and holy lives before You, Almighty God. Amen.

Meditation:
Partnership in Christ is a strong defense.

> Partnership in Christ,
> Strength for each new day;
> Triumphs and struggles
> Are along the way.
> Partnership in our journey,
> Sustained by loving prayer,
> Two hearts joined together,
> In the comfort of His care.

January 25

Inheritance

"To them God has chosen to make known among the Gentiles the glorious riches of this mystery, which is Christ in you, the hope of Glory." (Col. 1:27)

Christ in us. Father, what an awesome truth. You are everything we need to overcome life's ups and downs. Those tight spots that test our wills are only contests to prove great spiritual gain. When we say, "increase our faith," the crucible becomes hotter. Because of grace, we can offer praise for Your tender and caring hand that controls the heat. We know that our hope is in You. We praise You, Father, for sending us Your Holy Spirit. We praise You for the hard lessons learned and the victories won. One day we will reign with You for all eternity. Prepare our hearts, dear Lord, to surrender all to You. Prepare our lives to live out our faith with boldness. Remove all the supports that we have trusted in and depended on until we can say, I love You, Lord; "My times are in your hands" (Ps. 31:15a). Amen.

MEDITATION:
Our greatest inheritance is Christ.

Overindulgence brings
Useless things...
Meaningless vanity...
Possessions admired...
Jealously guarded in hearts
Where empty treasure is stored.

Christ knocks...
Doors open...
Love enters...
True living begins...
Kingdom treasure is unlocked.

January 26

Everlasting Life in Christ

"What he opens no one can shut, and what he shuts no one can open." (Rev. 3:7b)

Father, thank You for Your gift of salvation. You are the Open Door to eternal life. Always You call; always You seek. Faithful Lord, Your Holy Spirit calls us forth to enter through Jesus Christ—"the way and the truth and the life" (John 14:6). May we not reject You and find the door shut that "no one can open." Heaven's opportunity is today's choice. Today, may we hear Your voice and receive You into our lives. For Your love "woos" us into an eternal relationship with the Father, and the Son, and the Holy Ghost. Amen.

MEDITATION:
Now is the best time to receive everlasting life in Christ. For we do not have any guarantee that we will be granted a moment beyond the one we breathe.

One Step at a Time

Jesus, take my hand;

It's me, a sinner, learning to stand.
I am no longer with the crowd,
Now I stand alone...
Desperately waiting
For a Friend to come along.

I feel all "funny" inside
As Your Spirit "woos" me on...
Encouraging me to take
One step at a time.

Fear rises like roaring,
Billowy waves
High above me.
Then I catch a glimpse
Of Your loving eyes
That gently say, *"Child, trust Me!"*

With hands so strong
And arms extended wide,
You cheer me on
With gifts of love and courage
Wrought deep inside.

I take my first step,
Then two or three more—
With penitent tears,
As I reach for You,
Your Voice gently whispers,
"Child, you have found the Open Door."

January 27

Endure Suffering

"Do not be afraid of what you are about to suffer...Be faithful, even to the point of death, and I will give you the crown of life." (Rev.

2:10)

In Your sovereignty and wisdom, You give us the grace to bear and endure afflictions and hardships. Pain is never wasted—never futile. Because Your love and great compassion never fail, we learn how to comfort others. Your great mercy channels our torrents of pain into deep pools of compassion toward others. When we suffer for Your Name's sake, we can rejoice knowing that Your perfect plan for each one of us is unfolding as we go from "strength to strength" (Ps. 84:7). Give us the grace to be faithful, grace to endure the race we run. Amen.

MEDITATION:
Sometimes we must endure suffering. Will we remain loyal and true to our Savior Jesus Christ, Who was obedient to His Father, even unto death?

We must endure; we bear His name…
Children of God, we profess, we proclaim.
Our faith rests in Christ, who remains
"Closer than a brother" (Prov. 18:24) all of our days.
When tested we still stand…
Grace holds us in our Father's hand.

January 28

God Reveals Himself

"You say, 'I am rich; I have acquired wealth and do not need a thing.' But you do not realize that you are wretched, pitiful, poor, blind and naked." (Rev. 3:17)

Lord, all of our "things" are useless and devoid of satisfaction compared to Your riches, our true possessions on earth. Your gifts of salvation, love, forgiveness, power, and a strong mind are lasting and genuine riches—gifts that reap a multitude of blessings on earth and in heaven. Gifts given to serve others. Thank You, Jesus, for revealing and imparting Your inexpressible gifts to us. Make my life count for Your name's sake. May contentment be my heart's attitude. Teach me to trust Your purpose and plan for my life. Amen.

Meditation:
When God is revealed to us, healing begins.

> Smugly wrapped in pretense,
> Hidden beneath layers of pain,
> Are emotions guarded...unfeeling...
> In need of a Father's healing.
> Ever so gently He comes and whispers:
> *Receive Life and begin to live...*
> *Life is full of meaning*
> *When I AM what YOU choose*
> *To receive and give!*
> As He sweeps through our hearts,
> We gasp at delusions revealed
> When sin is no longer concealed.

January 29

God's Spirit

"The fear of the Lord is pure, enduring forever. The ordinances of the Lord are sure and altogether righteous." (Ps. 19:9)

Lord, teach us healthy fear. Fear based on reverence toward You. Because of Your great love, our common ground is Christ in us, giving us harmony and unity. Teach us to guard our hearts, keeping our relationship with You pure. Rule our hearts lest we stumble and fall into evil ways. Amen.

MEDITATION:
Paralyzing fear is not of God..."but a Spirit of power, of love, and of self-discipline" (2 Tim. 1:7).

> All of God's gifts are good,
> Equipping saints to love.
> It is in loving that healing begins

And broken wings are mended…
Lifting us higher than majestic peaks,
Above sin's cruel domain.

※

January 30

The Costliest Investment

"'I will be a Father to you, and you will be my sons and daughters, says the Lord almighty.'" (2 Cor. 6:18)

Thank You for being our Father, a promise of eternal keeping, a promise of earthly giving. You've chosen us to be in Your family. What incredible love!—an invitation so grand. What a privilege to be called a child of God. To be in the family of God is to be a part of eternal kingdom investments. Investments that no earthly gain can match. Amen.

MEDITATION:
God made the costliest investment *in* us at the Cross.

I know that my Redeemer lives! (Job 19:25)
He paid the price!
God sacrificed
His only Son
That I might live…
What can I give?
But my life back to Him.

※

January 31

Jesus

"We give thanks to you, O God, we give thanks, for your Name is near; men tell of your wonderful deeds." (Ps. 75:1)

Father, thank You for Jesus. What's in a name? In the Name of Jesus is strength and hope and blessings for today—and eternal life.

Every thing we will ever need is found in Jesus. I am very thankful. Forgive my times of ungratefulness when my thoughts and concerns crowd out Your will and purposes for my life. Amen.

MEDITATION:
Jesus is as near as our breath.

> I believe in the incarnation…
> God visiting earth as man.
> I believe in the incarnation…
> One true God residing in hearts
> As the Father, the Son, and the Holy Spirit.

February 1

Adopted into His Family

"I will say to the north, 'Give them up!' and to the south, 'Do not hold them back.' Bring my sons from afar and my daughters from the ends of the earth—everyone who is called by my name, whom I created for my glory, whom I formed and made." (Isa. 43:6-7)

Thank You, Lord, that our identity is in Your name. What an inescapable thought! We were created for Your glory and given life by Your breath. May we complete the tasks that You give us, putting our shoulders to the wheel and rejoicing in the privilege of bringing glory and honor to Your name. Amen.

MEDITATION:
We have been adopted into His family and called by His name.

> We ask You, Lord,
> To direct our steps
> And strengthen our hearts
> As we pursue Your plan for us.

February 2

Submission to His Rule

"I, wisdom, dwell together with prudence; I possess knowledge and discretion." (Prov. 8:12)

Father, give us wisdom…where there is wisdom, there is prudence, knowledge, and discretion. Open our minds to learning and our hearts to understanding, giving us godly insights and perspectives. Give us courage to spiritually grow, cultivating those gifts freely given. Amen.

MEDITATION:
To manifest God's goodness and His nature requires a willingness to be spiritually stretched beyond our comfortable surroundings and familiar settings. God produces His good work in us to the degree of, and at the point of, our submission to His rule in our lives.

> Look beyond questions and trials;
> Look into God's unchanging face.
> Our Father's hand is upon us.
> All is well…stay in the race.

☙ ❧

February 3

The Tongue is Set Ablaze

"I will make my words in your mouth a fire and these people the wood it consumes." (Jer. 5:14b)

Father, give me boldness to speak Your truths. Grant me courage to share the message of Your saving grace according to the leading of Your Spirit. Your Word is medicine for the soul and health for the body. Your Spirit mends broken hearts. By Your Spirit we awaken to a new beginning. We are transformed. Amen.

MEDITATION:

When the tongue is set ablaze by the Holy Spirit, nothing can contain it.
>   Words tumble out…
>   A tongue set ablaze.
>   Hearts stir…ears hear…
>   As the Holy Spirit moves.

February 4

God's Word

"'Is not my word like fire,' declares the Lord, 'and like a hammer that breaks a rock in pieces?'" (Jer. 23:29)

Yes, Lord, Your Word burns in our consciences, convicting and destroying sin in our lives. We stand before You broken, asking for mercy, forgiveness, and healing. You hear our cries and deliver us from our perilous sin. We come before Your throne of mercy. Your Word exposes our inner secrets and restores our heavy hearts—hearts weighed down with burdens and transgressions. Casting our cares upon You, we stand before You cleansed and free of our earthly burdens. Amen.

MEDITATION:

God's mighty Word purifies our decadent souls.

>   Forceful whishes of mysterious wind,
>   Encircling repentant hearts of sin…
>   Sweeping clean sin's debris,
>
>   Inviting Peace to live with thee.

February 5

Reservoir of Grace

"From the fullness of his grace we have all received one blessing after another. For the law was given through Moses; grace and truth came through Jesus Christ." (John 1:16–17)

Dear Father, how wonderful You are! No one can fathom or measure Your mercy and grace extended to us…grace that is abundant and available every day, every hour, every moment. Your grace is sufficient—a healing balm for every trial, every circumstance, every test. Receive my song of praise. Your love is staggering to my senses. Amen.

MEDITATION:
God's bottomless reservoir of grace sparkles with hope and flows freely.

> The coolness of His grace
> Against my grief-stricken face
> Quickens hope deep within
> That pain cannot erase.

∽§ §∾

February 6

Yielded to God

"No longer will they call you Deserted, or name your land Desolate. But you will be called Hephzibah [meaning 'my delight is in her'], and your land Beulah [meaning 'married']; for the Lord will take delight in you, and your land will be married. As a young man marries a maiden, so will your sons [or 'Builder'] marry you; as a bridegroom rejoices over his bride, so will your God rejoice over you." (Isa. 62:4–5)

You have infused Your Holy Spirit into our bodies. You take delight in us and rejoice over Your children. With loving gentleness, Your hand smoothes our rough spots. We are placed in a fertile and fruitful land. May our wills be pliable in Your mighty hand so that You may produce a bountiful harvest in us. Thank You, Lord, for being so desirous of us. Amen.

MEDITATION:
A life yielded to God bears earthly fruit and eternal reward.

Our life purpose is to be a fertile field for God

to cultivate. In His beautiful design, He has chosen us to become instruments for a great harvest. For reasons we cannot comprehend, we are entrusted with God's plans, purposes, and missions. Because we are highly esteemed by God, significance and great worth are given to us. Assignments are dispatched, empowerment given, and eternal reward granted.

February 7
Christ in Us

"'As for me, this is my covenant with them,' says the Lord. 'My Spirit, who is on you, and my words that I have put in your mouth will not depart from your mouth, or from the mouths of your children, or from the mouths of their descendants from this time on and forever,' says the Lord." (Isa. 59:21)

Put Your Word in our mouths, O Lord. When we are tempted to be discouraged, or to become despondent, recall to our minds Your Word. You are our God; we are Your people. Your signature is on our hearts forever. Give us ears that hear Your truths and sensitive spirits willing to do Your will. Amen.

MEDITATION:
Christ in us is to be shared.

> Empty people blankly staring…
> Looking for love to come their way.
> We pass them by and do not tell them—
> God is love and His love will stay.

February 8
The Name of Jesus

"I have given you authority to trample on snakes and scorpions and to overcome all the power of the enemy; nothing will harm you." (Luke 10:19)

Father, supernaturally, Your power flows through us. We are indwelled with Your Spirit. It's the same power that raised Jesus from the grave. We pray, Lord, that You might be glorified as the Holy Spirit seeks to do Your will through us. Give us a spirit of boldness and confidence in Christ as we take our stand against the evil one and all his cohorts—standing after we've done all that we can. Strengthen us as we take our stand, in Jesus' name, against the evil one and all his cohorts—trusting Your strength and wisdom to keep us standing. Amen.

MEDITATION:
The name of Jesus overcomes every foe.

> We make decisions every day…
> Follow Christ?
> Or go our own way?
> Though the road is rough
> And the way is winding…
> Jesus' love is worth finding.

ఌ ঌ

February 9
Harrowing Passageways

"When you pass through the waters, I will be with you; and when you pass through the rivers, they will not sweep over you. When you walk through the fire, you will not be burned; the flames will not set you ablaze." (Isa. 43:2)

Father, thank You for reminding us that we "pass through" our trials and that You are right with us—comforting us, encouraging us, and strengthening us. You bring comforters our way, sojourners on the walk of faith. In unexpected places we find Your faithfulness. You remain with us always. We are never out of Your reach. We are never asked to bear more than we are able. Amen.

MEDITATION:
When we pass through the harrowing passages of life and trust that God is in control, we can have His peace in the middle of very trying situations. We become stronger and our

hearts gain a greater capacity to love. Trials are often the very tools that God uses to develop our dependency on Him.

> Frightful feelings leap about;
> Anxious thoughts alarm.
> God is in every moment;
> He knows exactly what to do!
> Yes, stretching can be painful,
> But He is in the stretching, too!

February 10

Press In

"When I am afraid, I will trust in you. In God, whose word I praise, in God I trust; I will not be afraid. What can mortal man do to me?" (Ps. 56:3–4)

Who do I put my confidence in? I will trust You, Lord; I will submit my life into Your tender care. Guard my heart, Lord; may my focus be on You. Keep me attentive and obedient to Your leading. Your Word is a healing ointment and brings merriment to my heart. Fear brings torment; faith brings peace. With Your hand firmly resting upon the shoulder of Your Child, I need not fear man. For Your promises uplift my soul and still the inner storm. You are my encouragement both day and night. To You I turn, O Lord. Amen.

MEDITATION:
 The closer we press in to God, the farther away we are from self-complacency.

> Let's not be smug
> And remain alone,
> Without a Guide
> To call our own.
> The mistakes we make…
> Only God can erase.

February 11

His Divine Imprint

"The Lord within her is righteous; he does no wrong. Morning by morning he dispenses his justice, and every new day he does not fail, yet the unrighteous know no shame." (Zeph. 3:5)

Father, You are just and faithful! Forgive us when we blame You for the sin in our lives. Shape our thought patterns to reflect Your thoughts. Mold us into Your nature until we have a fountain inside us that overflows with Your goodness—a fountain of love, joy, peace, and trust—summoning people to taste the goodness of our Lord. Our Potter's hand is busy at the wheel of delight and holiness, restoring lives for His glory. It is You Who take such delight in us. Each morning breaks forth with Your gifts of justice and faithfulness. Let our souls dance with joy in Your presence, as we sing songs of praise. Amen.

MEDITATION:

Our tireless Potter perfects His people into holy vessels bearing His divine imprint.

> Touched by God…
> An everlasting imprint!
> A memorable moment…
> Divine intervention.
> Bearing His name,
> We are called His children.

⁂

February 12

His Love Lifts Us

"Do not gloat over me, my enemy! Though I have fallen, I will rise. Though I sit in darkness, the Lord will be my light. Because I have sinned against him, I will bear the Lord's wrath, until he pleads my case and establishes my right. He will bring me out into the light; I will see his righteousness." (Micah 7:8–9)

Your loving hand, Father, keeps us safe from our enemies' encroachment. You never fail. Your mercy and compassion restore us, giving us songs of rejoicing. Though we are crushed, You will lift us up. Even in our hour of peril, when we walk in the shadow of darkness, You are there. Your light dispels our fear. Deliver us from all of our enemies. In Your everlasting arms, we find comfort. Yes, our light and hope are found in You. Amen.

MEDITATION:
When we are enveloped in God's love, our enemies do not distract us. His love lifts us above our adversities.

>Though opposition assails me
>And the enemy begins to advance,
>Staunchly I take my stand,
>Dependent on God's strength—
>Knowing the battle is His to grasp!

February 13

Lion of Judah

"Surely the Sovereign Lord does nothing without revealing his plan to his servants the prophets." (Amos 3:7)

Dear Father, I am amazed at Your Sovereignty. You are so powerful and profound, and yet Your plan of salvation for mankind was made so simple that everyone could receive Your gift with childlike trust in You. Thank You, Lord, for meeting us at our level of understanding and then quickening our hearts and minds to receive You. Inside each heart You have sown seeds of desire. Water them, Lord, and bathe them in Your perfect will. Those seeds spring up with purpose and meaningfulness. For it is Your hand that made us and it is Your Spirit that blows on us. Strengthen us with Your Spirit. We glorify You, Lord, with praise and thanksgiving. Amen.

MEDITATION:
The Lion of Judah is our King!

Glorious Commander!
Lead the procession on…
Give us marching orders;
Let our fearful hearts be strong.
Exchanging fear for courage,
We go forth as called…
Marching to our victory song!

ﻌﮋ ﮊﻌ

February 14
God's Answer

"As soon as you began to pray, an answer was given, which I have come to tell you, for you are highly esteemed. Therefore, consider the message and understand the vision." (Dan. 9:23)

Your Word edifies and encourages, lifting up those that are brought low. Lord, give us discernment. Sheep know their master's voice. Truth comes to pass; untruth falls to the wayside and is no more. Therefore, let us press into Truth and know the witness of Your Spirit. "Your word is a lamp to my feet, and a light for my path" (Ps. 119:105). Amen.

MEDITATION:
God's answer is the best answer to our problem.

Grant us ears to hear Your answer
And trust to receive Your wisdom.
Sheep who know the Shepherd's voice
Must spend time with the Master.

ﻌﮋ ﮊﻌ

February 15
Confidence

"Have no fear of sudden disaster or of the ruin that overtakes the wicked, for the Lord will be your confidence and will keep your foot from being snared." (Prov. 3:25–26)

O Lord, when my confidence is shaken, please steady my hands and my feet. You are my God; You are my source of strength and joy. Hold me up through all my trials and circumstances. Teach me to do my best and then to rest in Your total care. Help me, Lord. Stabilize my emotions and calm my fears. Amen.

MEDITATION:
"So do not throw away your confidence; it will be richly rewarded" (Heb. 10:35).

> People come and go;
> Change is taking place…
> What once was important
> Is now insignificant.
> But God is unchanging…
> His wisdom can't be surpassed.
> God remains the same forever…
> Eternal Love that lasts!

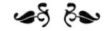

February 16

Double Portion

"Instead of their shame my people will receive a double portion, and instead of disgrace they will rejoice in their inheritance; and so they will inherit a double portion in their land, and everlasting joy will be theirs." (Isa. 61:7)

Only You, Father, could turn our former shame and disgrace into a bright and new beginning. Kingdom treasure is found in You. What the world offers, pales next to Your riches. There is joy in Your presence. Give us an undivided heart. Draw us closer, Lord, lest we wander. Deliver us from temptation. Amen.

MEDITATION:
When we turn our backs on folly and turn to God, He exchanges our waywardness for a "double portion" of blessing.

God waits for our return home…
And the Angels rejoice
When we come before His Throne.
Deeply He cares, deeply He calls…
O let's surrender all to our Lord!

ஒ ॐ

February 17

The Lord Bless You

"By faith Isaac blessed Jacob and Esau in regard to their future." (Heb. 11:20)

Dear Lord, let us be a blessing to our children. Teach us how to show them the love of Christ. Give us generous hearts when asked our advice or assistance. Anoint our children with Your eternal holy fire, drawing them to You. May they know how deep is Your love. Guard them and keep them close to You. And create in their souls a hunger and a thirst that only Your Spirit can quench. Amen.

MEDITATION:
"'The Lord bless you and keep you; the Lord make his face shine upon you and be gracious to you; the Lord turn his face toward you, and give you peace'" (Num. 6:24–26).

Dear Children,
May God richly bless you…
Give all your cares to Him.
Reach out and grasp the Truth.
Trust God… touch hope…
His Presence is within,
And love is His garment of care…
He leads you to pleasant places
And abundantly shelters you there.

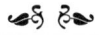

ஒ ॐ

February 18

The Good Fight of the Faith

"Let us fix our eyes on Jesus, the author and perfecter of our faith, who for the joy set before him endured the cross, scorning its shame, and sat down at the right hand of the throne of God. Consider him who endured such opposition from sinful men, so that you will not grow weary and lose heart." (Heb. 12:2–3)

Faith comes from You, Lord. When we weaken in our faith, You still are faithful. Perfect in us, Jesus, all that is dear to Your heart. May our gaze be steadily upward and focused on You as we daily take up our cross, counting it all joy because we bear Your Holy Name and are made in the image of God. There is "one Lord, one faith, one baptism" (Eph. 4:5). We honor You, Lord, and exalt Your holy name, for You are worthy to be praised. By Your grace, we fight the good fight of the faith. Amen.

MEDITATION:

There are many battles, many causes to defend, but only one fight is eternal: "the good fight of the faith" (1 Tim. 6:12).

>Weariness comes;
>We must press on.
>God gives us might…
>In Him we're strong.
>He will refresh
>His wearied saints.
>Looking upward,
>We will not faint!

⁂

February 19

The Transforming Power of God's Spirit

"I tell you the truth, wherever this gospel is preached throughout the world, what she has done will also be told, in memory of her." (Matt. 26:13)

Father, let my life exude the precious aroma of Christ. Tenderize those rebellious areas. Quiet my spirit. Your gentle voice says: *You are Mine, child; I have redeemed you. You bear My name. Abide in Me and walk in My Spirit. I am Your Father. I discipline My children because I love them. I will never leave you nor forsake you. Every good and perfect gift is from Me. I prepare your heart to receive gifts...gifts to share with others that will bring Me glory. Oftentimes the heart that is being prepared for My future glory experiences much pain and turbulence as the flesh resists My Spirit. Trust Me. Yield to Me. Your joy will be complete.* Father, may it be said about me that my passion is Christ. Amen.

MEDITATION:
No greater testimony is told than the transforming power of God's Spirit changing a depraved human heart into a Spirit-filled heart.

Such feeble attempts to gain power and fame...
There's One Who holds it all in His Name.
He chooses tasks for each of us to do.
Do you know Him? Does He spend time with you?

When quick answers seldom come,
Know that His plan requires work to be done.
What's important to Him, we may not understand.
Sometimes it goes unnoticed when it isn't our plan.

We work unto the Glory of God—
Whose wondrous gifts are planted within.
A bright day will dawn with jubilant joy
As God takes hold of our hearts of sin.

February 20

Attitudes

"[T]o be made new in the attitude of your minds." (Eph. 4:23)

Our life experiences and events are the tutors for our life lessons. How we respond to our life lessons determines the condition of our emotional well-being. Our thoughts affect our emotions and our actions. As we meditate on Your Word, our minds are being renewed. Father, remind us that a mind fixed on Jesus will produce peace in all of our circumstances, both in pleasant and unpleasant situations. Touch our minds, Lord, and renew our thoughts. May we reflect on Your love. Embraced by Your love, we are refreshed. Amen.

MEDITATION:

Our attitudes toward others ought to reflect Christ's grace toward us.

> Today we make choices that affect all of our tomorrows;
> Lord, fill us with Your wisdom to lessen the sorrows.
> O, Lord, create in us purity of mind, body, and soul;
> Quicken hearts to yield to the Spirit's renewal and control.

February 21

Every Promise...He Keeps

"You are my portion, O Lord; I have promised to obey your words." (Ps. 119:57)

Lord, today I press in closer. I want to know You. In You I delight. It is You who initiates love. You are here. Fill me with Your Spirit. Fill me with Your desires. May Your Word be on my lips and in my heart. Prepare me to serve You, O Lord, as I reach for Your hand of mercy and clasp Your hand of grace. Amen.

MEDITATION:
God keeps His promises. Are our promises a yes or a maybe?

God keeps every promise given,
Never revoking any of them.
Gifts of love and grace are offered,
Purchased by His Son.

Enter His gates of mercy;
Walk in fellowship with Him.
Welcome the *sweet Lord of grace*
Into our lives again.

February 22
Witnesses of God

"'I have revealed and saved and proclaimed—I, and not some foreign god among you. You are my witnesses,' declares the Lord, 'that I am God.'" (Isa. 43:12)

Father, help me to truthfully and zealously represent Christ in all that I say and do. Lord, make me a bold witness, telling others about Your power to rule, to save, to deliver, to teach, to instruct, to admonish, and to bless Your needy children. Let me share both momentous and painful times, remembering that You are "an ever-present help in trouble" (Ps. 46:1). You are a constant companion and friend. You, O Lord, are my strength and my joy. Amen.

MEDITATION:
Do our actions and words glorify God?

What I say I believe needs to hold true
During testing and tempestuous rule.
God is in every storm and sunburst noon,

Setting boundaries to fiery trials that consume.
He knows our frailties and mortal frames;
In tribulation He brings us great gain.

February 23

Think

"This is what the Lord says: 'Stand at the crossroads and look; ask for the ancient paths, ask where the good way is, and walk in it, and you will find rest for your souls. But you said, "We will not walk in it."'" (Jer. 6:16)

Lord, You ask us to examine ourselves before You, and to carefully and prayerfully seek Your counsel and guidance. Steady our feet, Lord, as we walk in the good way that You have prepared for us before our birth. You are the Way, and in You we will find rest for our souls. Our protection and provision come from You. Show us our divine assignments on the path of obedience; and as we sojourn, quicken our hearts to trust You. Guard and order our steps, Father, and watch over us. You are our peace, our strength, and our safety. We rest and hope in You, O Lord, within the counsel of Your watchful care. Amen.

MEDITATION:
Think before leaping.

> Impulsive hearts leap through doors of blind opportunity,
> Opening the windows of immediate gratification,
> To find empty rooms of wishful thinking.

February 24

Sincere Faith

"I have been reminded of your sincere faith, which first lived in your grandmother Lois and in your mother Eunice and, I am persuaded, now lives in you also." (2 Tim. 1:5)

Father, please help us to attain sincere faith and sincere love. Reveal to us any hidden areas where sin can cast a blight upon fruitfulness growing in our lives. May we grow and become a fruitful branch, clinging to the Vine in utter dependence, bearing much fruit. And when pruning is needed, help us to abide in You in confidence and trust. Cleanse us from our impurities and iniquities. Forgive us for our many doubts and anxious thoughts. Your compassion and mercy touch us, enabling us to stand. Amen.

MEDITATION:
Sincere faith lives for God.

> Our faith will be tested.
> How else will we know
> What lurks in our hearts,
> Where deception grows?
> With gentle pressure,
> He presses in...
> Our faith is measured.

ಌ ಔ

February 25

Responsibilities

"For this reason I remind you to fan into flame the gift of God, which is in you through the laying on of my hands." (2 Tim. 1:6)

Father, may the flame of prayerful intercession not be extinguished. Strengthen my commitment to come before You in prayer; convict me and burden me with the necessity of communion. Forgive me for the times when I allow prayer to be crowded out. Holy Spirit, You are the wind to the flickering flame. Shine brightly in my life, fulfilling Your purpose through me. Amen.

MEDITATION:
Knowing our responsibilities deafens our excuses.

In our love relationship with Christ, spending time together is of the essence, forsaking anything that would try to dominate us and seek first place in our lives.

February 26

Impurities

"Do not put out the Spirit's fire." (1 Thess. 5:19)

Ignite the fire burning in my heart, to a glowing blaze. Awaken within me all that gives pleasure to Christ Jesus, shaping me into a godly vessel. Shaping is *pressure by loving and merciful touch*, merciful fingers smoothing rough spots. May I not resist Your touch, O God. Consecrate me for Your Glory. I want more of You in my life and less of me. Amen.

MEDITATION:
Impurities are burned with holy fire.

Touch our hearts with fire
Ignited by the Spirit's breath.
Create in us Your desire
And know Your way is best.

February 27

Let Go

"For we are God's fellow workers; You are God's field, God's building." (1 Cor. 3:9)

May our lamps shine brightly, glowing with the Spirit, the oil of gladness. You plow the rough and rocky ground of our heart, preparing Your field for a great harvest. You invite all who are spiritually thirsty and hungry to come and taste Your righteousness, goodness, mercy, and wisdom. Lord, what is Your counsel for my life? Let me hear Your gentle Spirit's voice and obey

His leading that I might be effectual in Your hands. Amen.

MEDITATION:
To be used by God, we need to let go of self.

Open my heart to understanding, O God!

When I'm holding on to things too tightly,
Loosen my grip, Lord...
When thoughts are impure,
Tap me gently, Lord...

When fears and doubts steal joyful days,
And even simple things become hard,
Remind me, Lord, You wait on us,
And all You ask is that we trust.

Open my mind to truth, O God!

February 28

Christ's Apparel

"Therefore, as God's chosen people, holy and dearly loved, clothe yourselves with compassion, kindness, humility, gentleness and patience." (Col. 3:12)

Father, cover me with "compassion, kindness, humility, gentleness and patience." Molding, shaping, and forming is Your continual refining process. In weakness, I flinch; in Your strength, I go forward. Your redeeming love enables me to stand before You, clothed in *Your* apparel. Amen.

MEDITATION:
Are we as selective with putting on Christ's apparel as we are our own?

Attributes and virtues, when worn for Christ,

warm the hearts of many. We give from what has been given, not from depleted storehouses.

March 1

His Power

"But you will receive power when the Holy Spirit comes on you; and you will be my witnesses in Jerusalem, and in all Judea and Samaria, and to the ends of the earth." (Acts 1:8)

Father, thank You for the outpouring of the Holy Spirit. Your Spirit comes and lives are touched, lives are changed. I will sing and praise Your name in the Spirit. Renew the face of the earth, O God. Amen.

MEDITATION:
His power reaches the deadened parts of man, reviving him to wholeness.

> Words cannot express
> Our thankfulness...
> Manifest in us Your holiness.

March 2

Keeper of Our Souls

"He will have no fear of bad news; his heart is steadfast, trusting in the Lord. His heart is secure, he will have no fear; in the end he will look in triumph on his foes." (Ps. 112:7–8)

Nothing will happen to me today apart from Your knowledge and wisdom. Father, Your love embraces the small child within me. Help me to keep my thoughts on You and on Your love and care for me. You are sovereign, O Lord...You own the cattle on a thousand hills (Ps. 50:10). "[T]he whole earth is full of [Your] glory" (Isa. 6:3a). You give us Your peace. For, "You will keep in perfect peace him whose mind is steadfast, because he trusts in you" (Isa. 26:3). Your mercy and kindness purge our souls to cry out—Abba, Father. Amen.

MEDITATION:
Christ is the Keeper of our souls.

>Rest in God's care…
>Bring worry to His throne and leave it there.
>Do not doubt what He will do—
>Completely trust Him to provide for you.
>Read the Word and know Him well,
>Sparing self from needless anguish to tell.

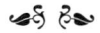

◅§ §▻

March 3

His Invitation

"The Spirit and the bride say, 'Come!' and let him who hears say, 'Come!' Whoever is thirsty, let him come; and whoever wishes, let him take the free gift of the water of life." (Rev. 22:17)

I thirst for You, O God. Fill me to overflowing with Your Holy Spirit. Immerse me continually in the water of life—baptizing me with the Holy Spirit and fire. Remove my impurities and iniquities, and place my feet on level ground, that I might not hear You say to me, "Yet I hold this against you: You have forsaken your first love" (Rev. 2:4). Amen.

MEDITATION:
God's invitation offers eternal life.

>God's invitation exacts commitment.
>His Spirit imparts strength and wisdom.

◅§ §▻

March 4

Serving

"'The King will reply, "I tell you the truth, whatever you did for one of the least of these brothers of mine, you did for me."'" (Matt. 25:40)

Lord, Your capacity to love all of mankind is love unspeakable… infinite love… undeserved love. And yet, according to

Your will and Your divine working through our lives, we receive unconditional love. We are made in Your image, glorious Lord. But reflecting Your nature is an ongoing process. We often disobey Your commands. Fear and selfishness take control and we begin to serve our emotions instead of You. Teach us to love and serve one another. Amen.

Meditation:
Serving is an outward sign of the heart's condition.

> There is only one way to serve,
> and that is to serve with excellence!
> Halfhearted or insincere attempts
> to serve God lack the glory due His name.

March 5

Faithfulness and Wisdom

"Call to me and I will answer you and tell you great and unsearchable things you do not know." (Jer. 33:3)

Lord, You've spoken a word of hope. We are invited to call to You—and You will answer our moans and cries of distress. Jesus, Your Word says that You will tell us great things—things our minds cannot comprehend apart from Your Spirit's revelation, answers we cannot find apart from the Holy Spirit's moving in our lives. Then we discover spiritual matters too wonderful to express. Amen.

Meditation:
God occupies our soul with His faithfulness and wisdom.

> God's Word satisfies soul hunger.
> Run to Him, there is no other.

March 6
Divine Purposes

"'Nevertheless, I will bring health and healing to it; I will heal my people and let them enjoy abundant peace and security.'" (Jer. 33:6)

O God, revive our smoldering dreams and heal our broken hearts. We are never out of Your reach. I praise You, Lord, for the healing rains of mercy and grace. We experience gifts of peace and joy, even in turbulent and deep waters, for everlasting Love comes to our rescue. Teach us to rely on You—taking one step at a time in faith (See Hebrews 11:1). Amen.

MEDITATION:
We are created for His divine purposes.

> It takes a Master Potter to remake a shattered pot of clay;
> And when He is finished, a new clay pot will be displayed.
> He fills us with spiritual gifts to minister in His Name;
> Humbled by His love, we will never be the same.

ക§ ൈ

March 7
A Timely Reply

"The Sovereign Lord has given me an instructed tongue, to know the word that sustains the weary. He awakens me morning by morning, wakens my ear to listen like one being taught." (Isa. 50:4)

Lord, give me "an instructed tongue" to encourage others. Let my words be few and weighed by Your Truth. Your Word keeps us energized and revived. Give us Your perspective. Take away distractions that prevent our ears from hearing. Amen.

MEDITATION:
A timely reply can color our world with hope.

> Choose your words carefully;
> You never know what will stick.

March 8

Infinite Love

"I cry out to God Most High, to God, who fulfills his purpose for me." (Ps. 57:2)

God, You are the strength of my heart. My heart would fail if it were not for Your infinite love. You are my strength and my shield. Your purpose prevails (Prov. 19:21). We have been called according to Your purpose (Rom. 8:28). We are priests and ambassadors in the name of Jesus Christ. Protect and strengthen us as we carry out, according to Your purpose and wisdom, those assignments given us. Amen.

MEDITATION:
His magnificent heart of infinite love captures our cry to God.

Captured by His tenderness,
Hearts cry out to God.

෴

March 9

God's Protective Circle

"As the Father has loved me, so have I loved you. Now remain in my love. If you obey my commands, you will remain in my love, just as I have obeyed my Father's commands and remain in his love." (John 15:9–10)

Your commands are not grievous; they protect us within the bonds of Your awesome love. Your love is pure, Father—mercifully it flows. Such goodness is hard to perceive. You've placed us in Your family. May Your love in us bear much fruit according to Your Word. "You did not choose me, but I chose you and appointed you to go and bear fruit—fruit that will last. Then the Father will give you whatever you ask in my name" (John 15:16). Teach us how to love one another as You love us. Amen.

MEDITATION:
There are consequences lived outside God's protective circle.

In every person's heart is a bent toward destruction and rebellion. With God's help, we can flee from the tempter's snares and remain in unbroken fellowship with the Holy Spirit.

March 10

Servants

"What, after all, is Apollos? And what is Paul? Only servants, through whom you came to believe—as the Lord has assigned to each his task." (1 Cor. 3:5)

Lord, nurture our budding lives to fully blossom. Cultivate servants' hearts. Bring to our remembrances those people You sent in our hours of need and the encouragement and comfort that followed. Thank You, Father. Amen.

MEDITATION:
We are Christ's servants.

Because Christ has created and chosen us for His divine purposes and reasons, submission to God is our emancipation from the bondage of self-importance.

March 11

His Eternal Reign

"First, I thank my God through Jesus Christ for all of you, because your faith is being reported all over the world." (Rom. 1:8)

Lord of grace, Your amazing love grows deep roots, giving us a strong and solid foundation to build loving and loyal relationships on. Help us become imitators of Your mercy, supporting and comforting one another in times of trial. Amen.

MEDITATION:
God sends His love to brighten our days.

> Windows of our soul
> Shimmer with gold…
> He Who is faithful,
> Radiates pure light.

∽§ ҈∾

March 12

What God Has Set Apart

"Know that the Lord has set apart the godly for himself; the Lord will hear when I call to him." (Ps. 4:3)

Lord, greatly are we esteemed. Find delight in us, O God. May we grow in carrying the Victor's torch of *new life* in Christ to a lost world of darkness. Amen.

MEDITATION:

No man can take claim to what God has set apart for His highest good.

> One by one, God calls,
> *"Come and know My love,*
> *Love won by drops of blood.*
> *Trophies…Polished by fire…*
> *Set apart for My highest good."*

∽§ ҈∾

March 13

The Father's Heart

"'Abba, Father,'" he said, 'everything is possible for you. Take this cup from me. Yet not what I will, but what you will.'" (Mark 14:36)

Abba, Father, may Your will be done. The Christian life is lived through. When decisions are painful to make and the mental fog inhibits our reasoning, give us clarity. When storms blow and howl, screeching a shrill pitch in our hours of darkness, steady our frames and quiet our souls. Amen.

Meditation:
To know the desires of the Father's heart, we first must know the Father.

> Friends remain friends
> During life's trials
> And celebrated joys.
> Friendship with God
> Stands the test of time.

March 14

Almighty God

"Find rest, O my soul, in God alone; my hope comes from him." (Ps. 62:5)

O God, rest comes as we quiet our hearts before You. In quietness and in confidence, we find hope in Your unfailing love and goodness. Do we stand naked before confessing fears and cares? Our guilt? Our shame? O Lamb of God, draw us nearer. Amen.

MEDITATION:
We slumber against the breast of Almighty God and receive rest for our weary souls.

> When slumber has ended,
> A new dawn has appeared.
> Resting in God
> Drives away our fear.

March 15

No One Like Him

"Your righteousness reaches to the skies, O God, you who have done great things. Who, O God, is like you?" (Ps. 71:19)

Father, nothing surpasses Your beauty or greatness. You dispense love and compassion. You defend the weak and oppressed, defeating their foes. Your plans and purposes never fail. O God, You are a constant and present helper and friend. You are our refuge, a mighty tower of strength. Amen.

MEDITATION:
Earth has nothing that compares to God's glory.

> Who is worthy to be compared to Almighty God?
> And what does Earth have that could equal God's glory?
> He competes with no one. Before the world was created,
> He existed in perfection. There is no one like Him.

March 16

Stay on Track

"The Lord will make you the head, not the tail. If you pay attention to the commands of the Lord your God that I give you this day and carefully follow them, you will always be at the top, never at the bottom. Do not turn aside from any of the commands I give you today, to the right or to the left, following other gods and serving them." (Deut. 28:13–14)

Your commands protect us, O God. May we not be foolish and spurn Your counsel. Because of Your great love toward us, we are taught and guided by Your Spirit working mightily in us. With thankful and grateful hearts we proclaim and boast in Your resurrected power through Jesus Christ our Lord. Amen.

MEDITATION:
Stay on track and receive His crown of faithfulness.

> God desires to crown us with many blessings.
> Remaining close to God provides every opportunity
> for His grace and power to be manifested in

our lives.
Staying on track in the spiritual race has great reward.

March 17
Our Gardener's Love

"Make a tree good and its fruit will be good, or make a tree bad and its fruit will be bad, for a tree is recognized by its fruit." (Matt. 12:33)

In what condition do You find our *temple* or body? Do we nourish our bodies with Your Word and cleanse our bodies with confession? Do we exercise our spiritual muscles as we stretch our faith? Are we a green, living tree with deep roots? O God, these are the questions our minds need to ponder. Amen.

MEDITATION:
Let's delight in our Gardener's love for us; we are the fruit from His tree.

Our family tree should be easily identifiable as belonging to Christ and having the familial traits of our Messiah.

March 18
Our Inherent Sinful Behaviors

"Put to death, therefore, whatever belongs to your earthly nature: sexual immorality, impurity, lust, evil desires and greed, which is idolatry." (Col. 3:5)

Father, You command us to "put to death" our sinful, idolatrous desires. May we, like Job, commit ourselves to You, vowing to keep our eyes on You and our hearts pure in Your sight, O God. May the power of Christ reign in our hearts. Amen.

MEDITATION:
Our inherent sinful behaviors, thoughts, and attitudes need to be crushed under the almighty hand of God.

Subdue us, Lord, with overwhelming love,
Grant us our Father's likeness from above,
As we deny our fleshly, lustful desires,
Becoming messengers of Your holy fire.

March 19

Unwavering Faith

"Therefore, since we have been justified through faith, we have peace with God through our Lord Jesus Christ, through whom we have gained access by faith into this grace in which we now stand. And we rejoice in the hope of the glory of God." (Rom. 5:1–2)

We rejoice in Your magnificent presence and look forward to Your second coming. Come Lord Jesus. May we receive Your Word in faith, putting to death unbelief. For Your word is marrow to our bones. Amen.

MEDITATION:
Unwavering faith gives way to rejoicing.

Our opinions are based on our thoughts,
Perhaps thoughts based on facts.
But God's Word is Truth,
Truth that remains "the same
yesterday and today and forever" (Heb. 13:8).

March 20

Clothed in Splendor

"But thanks be to God, who always leads us in triumphal procession in Christ and through us spreads everywhere the fragrance of the knowledge of him." (2 Cor. 2:14)

Holy Spirit, You working through us "spreads everywhere the fragrance of the knowledge of him." Let our lives be a testament of the glorious gospel of Jesus Christ. Come, Holy Spirit, and prepare hearts to receive God's Son. "Yet to all who received him, to those who believed in his name, he gave the right to become children of God" (John 1:12).

MEDITATION:
Christ is the sweet Rose of Sharon and the Lily of the Valleys, clothed in a splendor unequaled.

>   Look at the hills...
>   Where the wildflowers grow
>   Are windblown seeds
>   That multiply below,
>   All arrayed in splendid coats
>   Of spectacular rainbow color...
>   With brilliant faces all aglow,
>   Turned toward their heavenly Father.
>   What beauty can compare
>   To trusting seeds of faith?
>   Treasure is uncovered
>   In God's peaceful garden place.

ಌ ಌ

March 21

His Promises

"The wolf will live with the lamb, the leopard will lie down with the goat, the calf and the lion and the yearling together; and a little child will lead them." (Isa. 11:6)

You are the God of Peace, Lord of Perfection. "[Y]our kingdom come, your will be done" (Matt. 6:10a). One day we will live in perfect peace. "[F]or the earth will be full of the knowledge of the Lord as the waters cover the sea" (Isa. 11:9b). Amen.

MEDITATION:
Peace floods hearts inscribed with His promises.

God covers the earth with sovereignty and

timeless truth. He is above all other gods and one day will return for those who have put their faith in His Son.

❧ ☙

March 22

A Thankful Heart

"Give thanks to the Lord, for he is good; his love endures forever." (Ps. 118:1)

You are good, Lord. Rich is Your infinite love toward us! Holy is Your name. We give thanks, O Lord. We bow before You in worshipful praise, for You are worthy to receive honor and praise. We rejoice in Your goodness. Amen.

MEDITATION:
The attitude of a thankful heart is gratefulness.

> We demonstrate thankfulness
> with a servant's heart,
> doing unto others
> as Christ has done for us.

❧ ☙

March 23

God's Light

"This day I call heaven and earth as witnesses against you that I have set before you life and death, blessings and curses. Now choose life, so that you and your children may live." (Deut. 30:19)

Your voice spoke the world into existence. You are light in a dark world. Divine love is meant to be lived through You. Your love reaches a thousand generations. In You there are life and riches forevermore. Amen.

MEDITATION:
God's light creates a sunburst in our hearts.

We are the workmanship of God (Eph. 2:10),
A masterpiece designed by Him,
Softened with a "divine brush."
God's love is great towards us.

March 24

God's Peace

"But he said to me, 'My grace is sufficient for you, for my power is made perfect in weakness.' Therefore I will boast all the more gladly about my weaknesses, so that Christ's power may rest on me." (2 Cor. 12:9)

Father, Your power breaks through our weaknesses, exposing our thoughts, crumbling our independent attitudes. Break our stony hearts, Lord. Restore us. Remove our insecurities and fears. Unclasp our fingers that cling to "things." Rebuild our lives on the sure foundation of Christ Who is the Cornerstone. Amen.

MEDITATION:
A trusting heart is filled with God's peace.

God's peace rests on us;
Weak vessels are restored.
Glorious strength is manifested
In saints that trust His Word.

March 25

Esteemed

"A kindhearted woman gains respect, but ruthless men gain only wealth." (Prov. 11:16)

Dear Father, we are a walking testimony to everyone who crosses our paths. Our words and deeds are being observed. Grant our words and actions power to testify lives lived for and through Christ.

Lasting and genuine success and achievement are only accomplished through Your Son. Amen.

MEDITATION:

To be esteemed because Christ is working within us is a great honor. To acknowledge His intervention is Christ-honoring.

> Any mark made in this world is due to God's grace.
> He will crown us with His loving-kindness.

March 26

Love is Proclaimed

"Better is open rebuke than hidden love." (Prov. 27:5)

Father, may our tongue not delight in gossip or refrain from withholding truth. Grant us the compassion and courage to speak up when it is within our ability to do so. With motives that are pleasing to You, and after prayerful inquiry, let our words be Christ-honoring and our rebuke be expressed for the purpose of reconciliation and restoration. Amen.

MEDITATION:

Love is proclaimed with honesty and compassion.

> *Honesty* is a tender heart risking an unknown response and, yet, set free knowing that love speaks truth openly.

March 27

Relationships

"Discipline your son, and he will give you peace; he will bring delight to your soul." (Prov. 29:17)

We delight in the wisdom of Your mighty Word, O God. "And

the corrections of discipline are the way to life" (Prov. 6:23). Peace and delight are great spiritual riches. You are our hope for today and the deliverer of all our struggles. Amen.

MEDITATION:
Harmonious and pleasurable relationships create a calm and undisturbed state of mind.

> Godly mentors and role models are gifts from God.
> Godly input determines output.

March 28

The Mind of Christ

"If you are pleased with me, teach me your ways so I may know you and continue to find favor with you." (Exod. 33:13a)

Lord, "teach me your ways." Be my mentor and spiritual guide. Show me those things I do not know. Amen.

MEDITATION:
Having the mind of Christ means we seek to think and act according to His ways.

> To have the mind of Christ requires an intimate and personal relationship with Him. Knowing His Word helps us have spiritual insights as to what He would do in a given situation. His history speaks volumes.

March 29

Impure Motives

"For whoever touches you touches the apple of his eye." (Zech. 2:8b)

Father, evil that comes against us is powerless because You are our shield. And You, O Lord, will avenge those that are intent upon evil. Our pain pierces Your heart. We can agree with

Your servant Joseph, "You intended to harm me, but God intended it for good to accomplish what is now being done" (Gen. 50:20a). Only You can reconstruct the ruins. Amen.

MEDITATION:
God knows our hearts' impure motives. God sees our impure motives set forth in our actions.

> How many times did I strike His cheek with selfish actions that made Him weep?

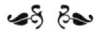

March 30

Trusting

> "I die every day—I mean that, brothers—just as surely as I glory over you in Christ Jesus our Lord." (1 Cor. 15:31)

Lord, do we die to self? Do we crucify our flesh and yield our bodies to the Holy Spirit's control? Do we have our way or do we fully submit to the leading of the Holy Spirit? Examine our hearts, O God. You will make a way for each one of us if we surrender *self,* allowing You to reign supremely in our lives. May today be lived in hopeful expectation of Your provisions for us. Lead me, Lord, to the summit. Let me achieve my full potential in Christ. Amen.

MEDITATION:
Trusting our gracious and beloved Lord means that we believe He is able to do for us what we cannot do for ourselves.

> Pride is self-destructive. We fail miserably when we choose independence and self-reliance. Dependence on the Creator is true success and security. For everything that we possess, all of our abilities, come from Him, "the author and perfecter of our faith" (Heb. 12:2).

March 31
God's Spirit

"How foolish! What you sow does not come to life unless it dies." (1 Cor. 15:36)

Lord, You teach us that we must be born again. This new birth is life in the Spirit washed by the Word. "For you have been born again, not of perishable seed, but of imperishable, through the living and enduring word of God" (1 Pet. 1:23). Amen.

MEDITATION:
God's Spirit penetrates our hearts with convicting power, exposing our sinfulness.

> Just like a seed put in the fertile ground grows,
> So does God's Word grow in receptive hearts.

ಊ§ ಕ∾

April 1
Our Portion

"[S]orrowful, yet always rejoicing; poor, yet making many rich; having nothing, and yet possessing everything." (2 Cor. 6:10)

Regardless of my circumstances, or whether I am poor or rich, "possessing everything" in Christ, I can rejoice. For our true riches are in Christ. We are princes and princesses of a royal priesthood. Amen.

MEDITATION:
With the Lord as our portion, our cup overflows.

> God's love never fails. His love is sufficient.
> Our cup overflows with His compassion and mercy.

ಊ§ ಕ∾

April 2

Sight

"We live by faith, not by sight." (2 Cor. 5:7)

Father, let Your Word continually wash over me, flooding and renewing my mind with Your truths and promises. Let faith supercede my limited sight. Amen.

MEDITATION:
Faith is continually rewarded; sight is its own reward.

> God is pleased with faith-filled hearts.
> He is interested in the eyes of our hearts (Eph. 1:18).

April 3

Release the "Old Self"

"Do not lie to each other, since you have taken off your old self with its practices and have put on the new self, which is being renewed in knowledge in the image of its Creator." (Col. 3:9–10)

Lord, keep me from the sin of spiritual complacency. Hasten my desire to meet daily with You. Teach me to lay aside all earthly distractions that compete with my quiet time of prayer and meditation. Thank You, Father, for patiently waiting and desiring to talk with me. Amen.

MEDITATION:
Release the "old self" to its Creator, and walk in newness of life.

> Releasing the "old self" that prevents us from
> experiencing our uniqueness in Christ, and
> putting on the "new self" quickened by Christ,
> opens doors of divine appointments and opportunities that have His imprint.

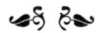

April 4

His Peace

"Peace I leave with you; my peace I give you. I do not give to you as the world gives. Do not let your hearts be troubled and do not be afraid." (John 14:27)

O Lamb of God, thank You for Your gift of peace. Give us the strength to receive Your peace and to respond trustingly in every situation, with the knowledge that You go before us and are always with us. Renew our minds, Precious Savior, with Your thoughts and truths, and grant us the grace to respond as ambassadors of peace and wholeness. Amen.

MEDITATION:
God sent His Peace and waits for open hearts to receive Him.

> The soul weeps for God's touch.
> The heart and Spirit of God is
> moved by our entreaties.
> God's Spirit touches heaven.
> Power explodes deep inside,
> and we are free.
> Our world lights up with hope.

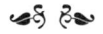

April 5

Healing Balm

"When anxiety was great within me, your consolation brought joy to my soul." (Ps. 94:19)

How reassuring it is, Lord, to read Your Word and discover that we are experiencing and feeling many of the same emotions that Your people did two thousand years ago. You are the same God—God without change! You will deliver us from our fears. Amen.

MEDITATION:
The ache in our souls requires God's healing balm.

Softly He comes without warning,
Quieting wrenched hearts of mourning,
Exchanging our sorrow for love.
Healing comes in fulfillment
Of His faithful, glorious love.

April 6

The First Step

"How great is the love the Father has lavished on us, that we should be called children of God! And that is what we are! The reason the world does not know us is that it did not know him."
(1 John 3:1)

Father, great is Your love. You drew me to Yourself, melting my stubborn heart of selfishness and indifference. Your Spirit entered into my heart, and now I am Your Child, reborn. Amen.

MEDITATION:
God takes the first step toward loving us.

God's extravagant love cost Him everything.
Poured out fury pummeled Jesus' body unto death.
Sin's payment was met when Christ was crucified.
And lavish love is given, because He lives.

April 7

Trust Has Eternal Rewards

"In vain you rise early and stay up late, toiling for food to eat—for he grants sleep to those he loves." (Ps. 127:2)

Father, You watch over us, even as we sleep. The blessing of a good night's sleep is restorative to our souls. Generously and graciously, You parcel out blessings to us, even when we are unaware of such good gifts. We cannot worry and trust at the same time. One must make room for the other. Teach us, O Lord, to reserve room in our hearts for trust to enter in and take up residence. Amen.

MEDITATION:
There is no value in doubt, but trust has eternal rewards.

> Legs are shaky,
> Eyes are swollen…
> Tears fall from our eyes.
> Voices fight against what's right,
> Attempting to shut out God's replies.
> Hold on tight; keep up the fight,
> For Trust is trying to be stolen.
> Doubt struggles, but loses—
> You're the one that chooses.
> The Commander is on your side!

April 8

Trust and Obey

"If you are willing and obedient, you will eat the best from the land" (Isa. 1:19)

Lord, Your promise requires hearts and minds to be willing and obedient to serve You. Pure hearts yielded to Your holy Word. Believing means trusting You. With longsuffering, You teach us life lessons. Patiently You wait and watch us grow. Even though it grieves Your heart, discipline is given to Your children. Your faithful provisions are plentiful; grant us believing hearts to receive. Amen.

MEDITATION:
We are given freedom to trust and obey.

> Why choose our own way?
> Live life abundantly with Him.
> God's love is reflected on faces
> Bathed in His powerful graces.
> Choose freedom to trust and obey.

April 9

The Supremacy of God

"I will meditate on all your works and consider all your mighty deeds." (Ps. 77:12)

Lord, bring to my mind the beauty and joy of Your creation. With breathtaking color You've designed the heavens and the earth. Rainbows color the skies…majestic mountains and deep seas cover the earth. Your goodness no one can fathom! Your faithfulness is forever. Amen.

MEDITATION:
The supremacy of God is power unequalled.

> Only God can redeem a soul. Only God can paint a sky.
> Only God can give purpose and meaning to life.
> Only God can reveal all the mysteries to the universe He created.

April 10

O Lord!

"You are the God who performs miracles; you display your power among the peoples." (Ps. 77:14)

You perform miracles. The miracle of life…the miracle of healing…the miracle of friendship…the miracle of sowing and reaping… the miracle of love between a man and a woman…the miracle of restoration…and the best miracle of all—the miracle of salvation. Amen.

MEDITATION:
We marvel at Your ways, O Lord!

> His mark is indelible on our minds and hearts. His visit leaves a permanent touch that forever alters our way of thinking. Recorded on the tablets of

our hearts are extraordinary events. And glory is given to God every time we tell our stories.

April 11

Great Pleasure

"[T]he Lord delights in those who fear him, who put their hope in his unfailing love." (Ps. 147:11)

Dear Lord, thank You for delighting in Your children. Those who trust You, O God, and know Your unfailing love are filled with hope. For You are love, and love gives us hope; hope gives us strength, and strength sustains us. Your mercy gives us wholeness and we are filled with Your joy! Amen.

MEDITATION:
Respect and honor given to God give Him great pleasure.

To esteem God in one's own heart and mind opens channels of love for His great display of power! And trusting Him increases the flow.

April 12

Beyond Our Imaginations

"In the same way, after the supper he took the cup, saying, 'This cup is the new covenant in my blood, which is poured out for you.'" (Luke 22:20)

Father of purity, perfection, and holiness, You drank the cup filled with the vileness of humanity. And in return, we have received Your promise, written in blood, as payment for our sins. Precious Lamb of God, we bow to You in thanksgiving for Your unfathomable mercy. Amen.

MEDITATION:
His love is beyond our imaginations—love that our hearts cannot fully grasp.

> Holy is our Lord…
> Beauty adorns His throne;
> Steadfastly we will minister,
> Until He calls us home.

April 13

Freedom

"You, my brothers, were called to be free. But do not use your freedom to indulge the sinful nature, rather, serve one another in love." (Gal. 5:13)

Lord Jesus, You are our example of love. Teach us how to love with a servant's heart of compassion and mercy. Let Your love flow through us, touching others as You have touched us. Show us how to bless one another, revealing Your great love for us. Guard us against busyness becoming a stumbling block to loving one another, as You have commanded. Amen.

MEDITATION:
Do not use freedom as a canopy for greed.

> In the shelter of God we are kept safe. He watches over us. We are always in his presence. We must learn to inquire of Him. Principles permeate His living word, and conditions must be met to obtain many promises—promises designed for guidance and provision. Our Liberator, Christ, delivers us from the bondage of sin. We are free to love one another.

April 14

He Is God

"My son, do not forget my teaching, but keep my commands in your heart, for they will prolong your life many years and bring you prosperity. Let love and faithfulness never leave you; bind them around your neck, write them on the tablet of your heart." (Prov. 3:1–3)

Father of faith, thank You for Your instructional teachings to help us grow in the knowledge of our Savior. Because of Your great *love and faithfulness*, every perfect gift from above is initiated by Your benevolent hand of mercy. Cultivate in us, O God, *love and faithfulness* that we may influence our corner of the world for Your name's sake. Amen.

MEDITATION:
Flee the temptation to doubt God's incomprehensible plan of love. Simply know that He is God.

Faithful Father from above,
Our Pavilion filled with love…
Fill thy cup with love divine,
Faithful Father, Friend of mine.

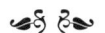

◈ ◈

April 15

Creation

"For by him all things were created: things in heaven and on earth, visible and invisible, whether thrones or powers or rulers or authorities; all things were created by him and for him." (Col. 1:16)

Lord, we are Your creation made in Your image for Your highest good. You hold the universe in Your mighty hand. How great You are, O God. Your hands made me and formed me. Give me understanding that I may learn Your commands and live for You. Amen.

Meditation:
All creation declares Your majesty!

> How magnificent Your vision must have been
> To take a brush and sweep across the glen,
> Arranging patterns across purple skies,
> Giving stars a place to shine and hide.

April 16

We Give Our Very Best

"And whatever you do, whether in word or deed, do it all in the name of the Lord Jesus, giving thanks to God the Father through him." (Col. 3:17)

Father, we are Your workmanship, and by the power of Your name, we have sufficient strength to carry out those tasks assigned to us. Blessed Lord, we give You thanks for making us ready to be used in Your kingdom work and for the good pleasure You seek in our imperfect jars of clay. Amen.

MEDITATION:
Jesus is the reason we give our very best.

> My Savior lives! How blessed I am
> To fellowship…to be His lamb.
> When I am weary, He holds me high;
> Tenderly He sings a lullaby.
> For in His arms of warm embrace,
> Are sufficient love and abundant grace.

April 17

His Gift of Service

"Whatever you do, work at it with all your heart, as working for the Lord, not for men, since you know that you will receive an inheritance from the Lord as a reward. It is the Lord Christ you are serving." (Col. 3:23–24)

Lord, bless and establish our hands as we offer them as a sacrifice unto You. For every gift of service You give us is an assignment authorized and endorsed by You. Divine tasks bear Your signature. We are Your entrusted messengers reflecting Your love. Amen.

MEDITATION:
His gift of service spurs us on to higher ground.

> Everything we do in Jesus' name
> Satisfies our Savior's claim:
> God's workmanship glorifies His Son
> When hearts of obedience have been won.

April 18

Choose to Obey

"Whether it is favorable or unfavorable, we will obey the Lord our God, to whom we are sending you, so that it will go well with us, for we will obey the Lord our God." (Jer. 42:6)

Lord, set my will in the direction of Your commands. Help me to reach for You, holding on to faith in the valley or on the mountaintops. Keep my feet on level ground; bring me to Your desirous place. Amen.

MEDITATION:
When we choose to obey, God's will is in motion.

> God knows the times and seasons
> For the revealing of His plan—
> And I can find comfort and rest
> In the hollow of His mighty hand.
> Now, Lord, grant me courage
> To take my first wobbly step;
> And when my journey is finished,
> In Your presence I will be kept.

April 19

God's Word Brings Order

"Your statutes are my delight; they are my counselors."
(Ps. 119:24)

Lord, I delight to know Your Word. Give me understanding, God, as I meditate on Your Word. Help me apply Your truths to my heart, knowing that Your Word is a healing balm to my soul. Keep me from willful neglect of Your Word, for in Your Word are promises of strength, renewal, healing, and redemption, wrapped in Your love and presented as gifts, "showers of blessing" (Ezek. 34:26) from Your omnipotent hand. Amen.

MEDITATION:
God's Word brings order to a confused mind.
> Our steps are ordered from above.
> His Word is sent; His Word is love.
> Many surprises are tucked away...
> One by one they enter our day,
> Refreshing us in abundant ways.

April 20

A Personal Relationship with Christ

"They are not just idle words for you—they are your life."
(Deut. 32:47a)

Lord, You are my life—and with Your Word inside me, my soul is fed. Revive me to wholeness and completeness, dear God. Your Word counsels me and directs my paths according to Your good will and purpose for my life. You long for an intimate relationship with Your children...restore us to You. Illuminate my mind with wisdom, knowledge, and an obedient and submissive spirit. Speak to me, Lord, for Your counsel is my daily bread, satisfying and filling my hungry spirit. Amen.

MEDITATION:
Life is built on the sure foundation of a personal relation-

ship with Christ.

> The emptiness in our hearts begins to stir
> Unregenerate man to search His Word.
> God's quickening Spirit gives life to all
> Who hear and receive God's call.

April 21

His Infinite Love

> "I broke the bars of your yoke and enabled you to walk with heads held high." (Lev. 26:13b)

Alleluia! We are free! Lord, let us use our freedom to take hold of Your mercy, shunning every evil that assaults our minds and bodies. Teach us, Lord, to walk in victory, "heads held high" as we take our marching orders from You. Lead us on heaven's highway of agape love…love that emulates Jesus. Amen.

MEDITATION:
Alleluia! His infinite love swallowed up our shame and disgrace.

> God does not reserve any portion of His love
> for a later time…all His love is given to
> us…poured out and forever overflowing. Open
> wide your heart and receive from the Lord, for
> He is good!

April 22

Mercy Calls Us Forth

> "He went on to say, 'This is why I told you that no one can come to me unless the Father has enabled him.'" (John 6:65)

Dear Lord, we are called by Your saving grace into an eternal love relationship. Praise Your name for revealing to us this mystery of rebirth. Today, as many people hear about Your love—love that required You to die on a Roman cross for our sins—I pray that many hearts will receive You. "Yet to all who received him, to those who believed in his name, he gave the right to become children of God—children born not of natural descent, nor of human decision or a husband's will, but born of God" (John 1:12–13). Receive my prayer, O Lamb of God—our Risen King! Amen.

MEDITATION:
Mercy calls us forth and grace adorns us with His righteousness.

>His knock is gentle at the door of my heart;
>With persistence His love courts my senses.
>Apprehension and guilt pierce my soul;
>His love overwhelms me, washing me clean.
>And I am free, truly free within.

April 23

An Extended Hand

"...Freely you have received, freely give." (Matt. 10:8b)

Father, from Your extended open hand, we receive. The fullness of the earth belongs to You. Help us to be open-handed, generously giving to others what we have received from You, knowing that we are sharing what is rightfully Yours. Amen.

MEDITATION:
An extended hand, an invitation.

>An open hand says, *"Take and eat.*
>*Remember the Giver grants the feast."*
>He, Who delights in you, gives His best.
>Pray for laborers for Christ's harvest.

April 24

O Faithful Father, Your Grace is Given

"But when they arrest you, do not worry about what to say or how to say it. At that time you will be given what to say, for it will not be you speaking, but the Spirit of your Father speaking through you." (Matt. 10:19–20)

Gracious Father, Your grace is given to us as we need it, according to Your perfect timing and purpose. Daily Your love touches and equips our lives with wisdom, courage, and strength. Your Holy Spirit is our testament of the resurrected power of Christ, Who indwells believers. Amen.

MEDITATION:

His faithfulness must be grasped by trust. Once trust takes hold of God's faithfulness, our eyes are opened to His provisions.

> Trust is built and strengthened with severe
> testing and visited by many afflictions. God's
> Comforter sustains us and walks alongside.
> Faith acknowledges God's Companion and
> rests in the assurance of God's promises. Faith
> and Surrender meet, and we rest in Almighty
> God.

April 25

Our Daily Bread

"Why spend money on what is not bread, and your labor on what does not satisfy? Listen, listen to me, and eat what is good, and your soul will delight in the richest of fare." (Isa. 55:2)

Lord, You are our daily bread; Your Word is good to taste and is life to my soul. Satisfy my hunger with Your life-giving manna. Bring me under Your power of conviction when my soul is undernourished, and before my senses become dull. When I look into the mirror of my soul, let me see Your smile and then respond to Your sweet embrace. In the deep secret places of truth, may obedience rule over my flesh. Amen.

MEDITATION:
Our daily spiritual bread is not homemade—it is made of three persons in One.

> To partake of Divine Bread,
> Seek after One Who fulfills and satisfies…
> Taste and know that God is sufficient and faithful.
> And His spiritual riches will fatten your soul.

April 26

He Is Unchangeable

"Even in darkness light dawns for the upright, for the gracious and compassionate and righteous man." (Ps. 112:4)

Father, what promise of hope You give us: even in our darkness, light will burst forth for the righteous. You, O Lord, are our Promise of Light; bring us into a sunlit morning of communion with our Morningstar! Yes, dawn will break forth over the horizon, and a new beginning of promise will light up our lives with hope…eternal hope. Amen.

MEDITATION:
His light never changes, because He is unchangeable!

> Light piercing through the darkness
> Turns the darkness into glorious light.
> God's eyes are on us…
> We're never out of His sight.
>
> Though some things appear unjust
> And pain rides on pounding waves,
> Believe He Who designed you
> Knows when to provide an escape.

For "no temptation has seized you" (1 Cor. 10:13a)
Because God is in control;
Trust His timing and purpose…
Trust His way out, then go!

ఌ ॐ

April 27

Bountiful Riches

"May the Lord repay you for what you have done. May you be richly rewarded by the Lord, the God of Israel, under whose wings you have come to take refuge." (Ruth 2:12)

Lord, only Your rewards have eternal value—and blessings for today. You are our refuge and we are kept safe under Your wings of glory. Cover us with Your protection; may Your angels minister to us and encamp around us. Anoint our bodies, and send us out into the white fields to serve You zealously and wholeheartedly. Amen.

MEDITATION:
Bountiful riches come from our Father in heaven, Giver of Eternal Life, our Horn of Salvation.

It's His to give,
The Giver of Life,
Our Wounded Healer,
By His stripes.
Come as you are…
Pretend no more…
Give your life…
He will restore.

ఌ ॐ

April 28

Conversation of Faith

"But you, dear friends, build yourselves up in your most holy faith and pray in the Holy Spirit." (Jude 20)

Dear Lord, we must learn how to encourage ourselves and to seek spiritual growth through prayer and meditation. Teach us, Lord, to be persistent and zealous in working out our new lives in Christ Jesus. Pray through us, Holy Spirit, touching the earth with God's love and grace. Amen.

MEDITATION:
God delights in our conversations of faith—our communion with Him.

> Holy Spirit, take my prayer
> Before the Father's loving care.
> May beams of light from heaven descend
> To remind someone that He does mend.
> Breathe life in souls today,
> Seeking those who have gone astray.
> Precious Lord gently lead;
> Come beside us as a gentle breeze,
> Full of splendor, full of power,
> Our Savior, our strong Tower.

April 29

Glory or Dishonor

"Whatever your hand finds to do, do it with all your might, for in the grave, where you are going, there is neither working nor planning nor knowledge nor wisdom." (Eccl. 9:10)

Lord, thank You for Your wisdom. Whatever tasks we do, we are to do them in a way that is pleasing and honoring to You. Your principles guide, instruct, and illuminate our minds in the direction You desire us to go. Your Word, applied to our hearts, becomes like a protective life vest to insulate us as we navigate the dark, turbulent waters. Captain of our souls, teach us to abide in You and to serve with excellence. Amen.

MEDITATION:
All tasks given, according to God's will, are purposeful and

productive. How we choose to perform them either brings glory or dishonor to His name.

There's a job to be done—
Support it with prayer.
Give it your best—
God will meet you there!

🙠 🙢

April 30
Melodious Rapture

"'I will be found by you,' declares the Lord, 'and will bring you back from captivity.'" (Jer. 29:14a)

Thank You, Father, for rescuing me from the evil one's domain and delivering me from the fears that ensnared me. Your anointing breaks the bonds that grip us. When we are weak, You clothe us with strength. You give us a garment of praise, for You are merciful, O God! Secure in the safety of Your watchful care, we can attempt mighty things for our God Who grants us victory! Amen.

MEDITATION:
God's great love flows over all the land in melodious rapture.

Cords of love strike harmonious sounds.
Our Savior's song of deliverance resounds.

🙠 🙢

May 1
A Blessing from Our Father

"May the favor of the Lord our God rest upon us; establish the work of our hands for us—yes, establish the work of our hands."
(Ps. 90:17)

Father, direct us to the work that You have prepared for us to do. Grant us favor, Lord, instilling Your desires in our hearts. And as we work, let us labor joyously in our tasks, knowing that each step guided by Your hand brings us closer to Your divine plan and purpose. Give us endurance and patience, Lord, as we keep our eyes on You. Amen.

MEDITATION:
A blessing from our Father gives validation to the work of our hands.

> His Spirit moves our hearts to serve Him with
> thanksgiving, as we reflect on the greatness of
> His love towards us.

ଏହି ହେ

May 2
You, O Lord...

"Lord, you establish peace for us; all that we have accomplished you have done for us." (Isa. 26:12)

Yes, Lord, we boast in You. For You have done a mighty work in our lives. You ignite the spark that inflames our dreams and visions, our hearts' desire to grow in the loving glow of Your grace. You lead us along divine paths that bless and encourage us—paths of obedience that exact fiery refining and polishing. But, You, Lord are always with us. We give You the glory, O Lord. Amen.

MEDITATION:
You, O Lord, are able to do all things.

> You, O Lord, are the beginning;
> You, O Lord, are the end.
> You, O Lord, are Father;
> You, O Lord, are Friend.
> You, O Lord, carry us
> When we cannot stand.
> You, O Lord, move heaven and earth
> When You hear Your children's prayers.

You, O Lord, take us into Your arms
And receive all of our earthly cares.

ಎಫ಼ ಓ

May 3

Perception

"As iron sharpens iron, so one man sharpens another."
(Prov. 27:17)

Dear Lord, help us to discover our spiritual gifts. Teach us to honor one another, remembering that You have made each one unique and have given us great value. Help us to use our gifts in Your family—the Body of God—that we may minister Jesus' love and strengthen one another. Let us not defile Your Body. Amen.

MEDITATION:
Our spiritual perception becomes clearer as we become more aware of God's greatness.

We will grow as we accept challenges and take
risks in doing the right things according to
God's principles.

ಎಫ಼ ಓ

May 4

Jesus' Love

"'Turn to me and be saved, all you ends of the earth; for I am God, and there is no other.'" (Isa. 45:22)

Lord, You are the only One to turn to. Only You can save us from eternal separation. The shed blood of Christ saves us from eternal damnation. You, O Lord, rule forever and ever. Rule in our hearts today and receive the glory due Your name. Amen.

MEDITATION:
Jesus covers the earth with brilliant colors; reflective rays of Christ's glory are like a rainbow of promise ushered into a formi-

dable sky.

> Pride keeps us from living the life we've been entrusted with;
> The way of obedience is a path of righteousness and joy in the Spirit.
> Willing hearts are open to God's counsel of love and correction…
> Submission honors Him.
> And when life on earth is finished, life in Christ lives on and on!

May 5

Stand for Jesus

"So he said he would destroy them—had not Moses, his chosen one, stood in the breach before him to keep his wrath from destroying them." (Ps. 106:23)

Merciful Savior, You are long-suffering and merciful. You intervene and seek people to intercede for countries and peoples, sparing them and us from destruction. You are faithful and just, therefore sin cannot be ignored. Amen.

MEDITATION:
When we stand for Jesus, we stand with Him and His heavenly host.

> Stand for Jesus!
> Shout on high!
> His Spirit is moving;
> His Spirit is nigh.
> We're in His mighty army,
> Willing to heed His call.
> To stand for Jesus,
> We must stand tall.

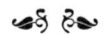

May 6

Christ's Invitation

"The Lord loves righteousness and justice; the earth is full of his unfailing love." (Ps. 33:5)

Glorious Lord, You are an endless reservoir of unconditional love—love that each one of us longs for. Creation is Your signature of purpose and destiny. Fill us, O Lord, and use us in Your kingdom, as You rule on earth and in heaven. Quicken lost souls with Your precious redeeming grace, saving them from spiritual death. Bring us into everlasting life. Amen.

MEDITATION:
Accept Christ's invitation and drink from the Wellspring.

The Invitation

An invitation to turn away
from all the evil of the day
pierced my heart… I gasped…
and with childlike trust I asked,
"Can I be forgiven of my past?"
He said, *"Child, I died,*
was buried, and rose again.
My shed blood purchased you—
With Me inside, You'll be brand new."
I'll live my life for you, Lord;
Give me strength, I pray, and
protect me from the evil of the day.

৵৽ ৻৶

May 7

Compassion

"A man of knowledge uses words with restraint, and a man of understanding is even-tempered." (Prov. 17:27)

Father, teach me to listen intently, with love and understanding, and to be slow to speak. Let my spirit be controlled by Your Spirit, bearing the fruit of Your generous love—love that isn't easily offended, love that looks to You for approval. Give me speech that honors You and a heart filled with Your love. Amen.

MEDITATION:
Compassion towards others will give us few regrets.

>   Compassion offered to a friend in pain,
>   soothes and medicates like good and timely
>   advice does for someone seeking wise counsel.

୶ଛ ଛ୶

May 8

Conversations with God

"As iron sharpens iron, so one man sharpens another." (Prov. 27:17)

Lord Jesus, in Your infinite wisdom You made us with a deep yearning inside to need one another. You draw us into Your loving arms, and by Your love we are blessed with friends. Your voice reawakens us. You satisfy our need to belong through the blessing of friendship. Yes, You place us in families—families that spiritually give us roots—and with mentors that give us encouragement and counsel as they mirror You. O God, You know our needs; in love and in faithfulness, those needs are met as Your strong right arm is moved by our entreaties. Glorious King, we praise Your holy name! Amen.

MEDITATION:
If our conversations with God aren't stimulating, we need to ask if God has had an opportunity to speak.

>   You long to hear from us
>   and wait for us to come;
>   We spill out selfish wants,
>   leave, only to return again.
>   Patiently, You listen…
>   but do You get to speak?

> Ah! Now there's silence
> The mind begins to seek…
> On bent knee, we ask thee
> To visit and share our week.

૭૬ ৡৢ

May 9

Mercy and Grace

"The Lord has vindicated us; come, let us tell in Zion what the Lord our God has done." (Jer. 51:10)

Father, because of the righteousness of Christ, our sins are forever buried. We have a sure foundation built on the Cornerstone that was rejected. Because of His obedience, we are made righteous. May we shout the victory song of praise. Christ works mightily transforming our lives in the beauty of His holiness. Amen.

MEDITATION:
Christ's mercy and grace define beauty.

> Unblemished beauty
> Purified…
> The Potter's touch
> Restorative…
> Everlasting value.

૭૬ ৡৢ

May 10

God's Faithfulness Triumphs over Evil!

"I will give the treasures of darkness, riches stored in secret places, so that you may know that I am the Lord, the god of Israel, who summons you by name." (Isa. 45:3)

Lord, give our ears the knowledge of Your sweet voice. "Look to the rock from which you were cut and to the quarry from which you were hewn" (Isa. 51:1b). Yes, Lord, we are Your children. We run to You; we seek Your face. And You, O God, are merciful, just, and compassionate! We will come forth as pure gold. In our trials, we will find You faithful. Come, Lord Jesus! Amen.

MEDITATION:
Darkness cannot spoil the deep treasures of God, for God's faithfulness triumphs over evil!

Secret Places

Conflict wars in the mind,
staunch and stubborn hurts that bind.
Locked inside festered sores decay;
kept a secret…darkness preys.
Come, Holy Light, search the room,
expose the pain, wash the wound.
Deal with us gently
And help us to forgive—
Free us from the sting of sin,
that we may truly live!
Break the powers of darkness
in the secret place;
And restore us to wholeness
by Your healing grace!

ಆ ಕ

May 11

His Treasure of Love

"Blessings crown the head of the righteous, but violence overwhelms the mouth of the wicked." (Prov. 10:6)

You honor us with many blessings—delightful surprises—surprises held in Your open hand! With loving faithfulness and mercy, You have stored up for us many treasures. You crown us with jewels that we lay at Your feet. Let us serve You, dear Lord, all the days of our lives. Amen.

MEDITATION:
Our poverty-stricken hearts become fattened with kindness and mercy when the Master fills our hearts with His treasure of love.

> We are of great worth to Almighty God. For reasons we cannot understand, He places great value on each one of us, even to the point of ransoming us with His life as payment for the vileness of mankind.

May 12

A Reflection of God's Provision

"Our people must learn to devote themselves to doing what is good, in order that they may provide for daily necessities and not live unproductive lives." (Titus 3:14)

Lord, You are the way to abundant living. Many times it means difficult labor and entering through unfamiliar doors of opportunity. But when we are fearful, we can trust in You. Make our lives count eternally, for Your name's sake, I pray. Teach us how to be a blessing wherever we are placed. We seek Your face, Lord, for guidance and direction. Amen.

MEDITATION:
We are a reflection of God's provision.

> Will we go through open doors
> or choose to walk away?
> Heads held high or chins down
> beneath the heavy sway?
> Trusting God in all we do
> will bring clear-cut paths;
> Serving Him brings joy to our tasks.

May 13

You May Get What You Crave

"For the love of money is a root of all kinds of evil. Some people, eager for money, have wandered from the faith and pierced themselves with many griefs." (1 Tim. 6:10)

Gracious Lord, whenever we worship anyone or anything and take our eyes off You, we are being controlled by the enemy. Keep us from dangerous enemy soil where many become subtlety deceived and allured by the things of this world. Our safety is only in trusting You. Forgive us when we fail to acknowledge thankfulness for all our many blessings. Give us generous hearts and willing hearts eager to share with others what we have received from You. Amen.

MEDITATION:
Be careful what you crave—you might get what you crave.

>   Lord,
>   Withhold cravings that would harm us;
>   Oh how foolishly we entertain them.
>   Fill us with pure love—heaven's dew.
>   And, in Your infinite wisdom,
>   Withhold longings not from You.

May 14

The Word of God

"As it is written: "He has scattered abroad his gifts to the poor; his righteousness endures forever."" (2 Cor. 9:9)

The power of Your Word, O God, restores and lifts us to higher ground. Your Word heals and encourages—revealing truth. With power and purpose, Your Word goes forth to fulfill and accomplish Your desires. Father, thank You for Your Word—a mighty spiritual weapon to tear down strongholds—to deliver and save us! Give us boldness. Teach us not to withhold what we have been taught, as we give forth the Word. Amen.

MEDITATION:
The Word of God is written; His love is inscribed on our hearts!

> Precious Lord, what can we give
> to wounded people everywhere?
> Disappointments, angry looks—
> all bound up in silent hurts.
> Smiles like bandages cover all,
> trying to hide the torment inside.
> Your transforming Word must be shared,
> telling others how much You care.
> Your love sets us free!
>
> What gift will last, O Lord, I pray…
> 'Tis Your Book of Truth…always.
> Read His Word; Hear His Voice;
> our Lord is speaking! O heart rejoice!
> Soul be still before our King,
> Who gives us a new song to sing!
> Peace does come when trust begins
> to believe in Him Who always wins!

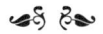

⁌ ⁋

May 15

Come to His Throne

"His splendor was like the sunrise; rays flashed from his hand, where his power was hidden." (Hab. 3:4)

Lord, You spoke and the universe was set in motion. One touch from You is life changing, and one blow upsets the plans of the wicked. Ruler of heaven and earth, shine brightly, casting heavenly light, the hope of eternal life on a sinful world. Amen.

MEDITATION:
Come to His throne and receive mercy and healing.

I'll meet You at our quiet place
where we can talk and slow the pace;
With see-through hearts and truthful lips,
eyes pour out tears to life's tugs and nips.
Comfort touches our grieving souls.
Once again, we've come home!

May 16

Our Life-giver

"The Sovereign Lord is my strength; he makes my feet like the feet of a deer, he enables me to go on the heights." (Hab. 3:19)

Lord God, You are my lifeblood. Recall to my mind that You are always with me. When I am afraid, teach me to trust You. And when emotions run their frenzied course, set me on higher ground, O Lord. You are my armor bearer; shield me from disaster, O God. Stay by my side. Amen.

MEDITATION:
Our Life-giver nourishes and nurtures His creation.

You are my confidence, O Lord—
The great I Am.
Take all my doubts, O Lord—
Exchange them for "I can."

May 17

No Firmer Foundation than Our God

"The Lord is good, a refuge in times of trouble. He cares for those who trust in him." (Nah. 1:7)

Lord, when we're tossed to and fro, may we stand in Your strength and take courage knowing that the battle is Yours. We are safe in Your protective custody. Give us Your victorious banner of sustaining power and grant us single-mindedness, that we may focus on

You. We take our stand and pledge our devoted love to You, Lord. Amen.

MEDITATION:

All God's promises are solid. There is no firmer foundation than our God.

Eyes of Love

I see you when the clouds are gray.
I see you in a sunlit day.
A rainbow of promise
colors the skies above…
Reaching the earth with My love.
There is never a moment
when you are out of sight.
I love you, My Child,
with great delight.
Storms will come; rivers will rise.
The enemy will taunt;
The enemy will lie.
But you are covered
with My protective eyes.

ꙮ ꙮ

May 18

His Design and Tender Love

"Through him all things were made; without him nothing was made that has been made." (John 1:3)

Creator of heaven and earth, gently You speak to us today. We hear Your voice through Scripture, in prayer, and as we look into the eyes of Your children. We hear Your voice in the silence and adoration of worship. Heaven and earth are Yours. Father, we are so grateful that You entrust us as stewards of Your creation. Keep us in step with the Holy Spirit as He produces fruit in our lives—fruit cultivated in Your vineyard and tenderly fashioned by Your hands.

Amen.

MEDITATION:
Listen for His voice in the splendor of His design and tender love.

> There is an unspoken language
> in the giving of His love;
> Resounding throughout the earth is
> a message from above.
> Come and share the sweet intimacy
> that He yearns to give today.
> Fill your cup to running over—
> Then give it all away.

May 19

Identify with Christ

"I am the Lord, your Holy One, Israel's Creator, your King." (Isa. 43:15)

Lord, You tell us Who You are. "I AM" says it all. Lord God, Creator of heaven and earth, our King—One who is personal, intimate, and powerful—we come before You with awe and we acknowledge Your presence. Your Word declares: "'You are my witnesses,' declares the Lord…'so that you may know and believe me and understand that I am he…'" (Isa. 43:10a). Give us spiritual sight, Lord. Open our eyes. Quicken our hearts to grasp the meaning of Your truth that by Your Spirit You are among us. Amen

MEDITATION:
When we identify with Christ, wholeness becomes reality.

> Give us unity and harmony;
> Bring us into agreement.
> Heal broken hearts;
> Restore bodies—renew.

Complete in us unfinished work,
Work that You have begun…
Fatten our souls for godly gain,
All to the glory of Your Son.

May 20

He Brings Everything We Need

"See I am doing a new thing! Now it springs up; do you not perceive it? I am making a way in the desert and streams in the wasteland." (Isa. 43:19)

You have made the way clear, Lord, in the hard places. God of miracles and impossibilities, God of dreams and restoration, God of hope and might, thank You, Father, for lifting our weary heads and putting a song of victory into our hearts as You lead us through life's perils. Lead us, our Shepherd; direct and order our steps. Amen.

MEDITATION:
When God enters our lives, He brings everything we need.

He makes a way for weary hearts,
Bringing comfort to a gentle start;
Knowing exactly what comes next,
He meets our every need confessed.

May 21

Praise

"The wild animals honor me, the jackals and the owls, because I provide water in the desert and streams in the wasteland, to give drink to my people, my chosen, the people I formed for myself that they may proclaim my praise." (Isa. 43:20–21)

Lord, we lift our voices of praise—in song, in dance, in spirit, and in quiet meditation and reflection. May people see within us the God of peace and joy. O Lord, remind us that our confidence is in You—

a confidence that is God-centered, not self-centered. We have the assurance that whatever comes against us You will use for our good. Therefore, in every circumstance we are able to have an attitude of joyfulness. Amen.

MEDITATION:
Our praise to Jesus echoes praise to the Father.

> Be delighted, O God, with the praise of Your
> people, devoted hearts rejoicing in Your mercy.
> For You continually intercede for us with
> loving vindication, intervening and battling the
> enemies of our souls.

May 22

Jesus

"'I, even I, am He who blots out your transgressions, for my own sake, and remembers your sins no more." (Isa. 43:25)

Lord Jesus, showers of mercy and grace are upon us as we receive Your forgiveness and are given a fresh start. Every moment contains a seed of promise. In every moment is a new beginning—the discovery of possibilities and opportunities as we seek Your face. Grant us hearts that are open and expressive as we rejoice with thanksgiving. Amen.

MEDITATION:
Jesus Christ erases our disgrace.

> Sinful pleasure…
> Purchased at a great price;
> Consciences deceived
> Are now alive in Christ.
> Great is His mercy;
> His favor covers all…
> Cleansing blood washes
> Aching hearts and souls.

Shame has no place where
Disgrace is erased.

ಆ ಈ

May 23
Promise Keeper

"They will say of me, 'In the Lord alone are righteousness and strength.' All who have raged against him will come to him and be put to shame." (Isa. 45:24)

Father, salvation and victorious living come from Your mighty right hand that goes before us. The blood of Jesus, incomprehensible love, saves us. Our lives are shaped by Your grace. Our souls take root as we apply Your principles to our daily lives. Giver of life, move mightily through us. All that we are or ever will become is established by You. In Your strength, we stand before You and accomplish those things You have determined. Amen.

MEDITATION:
Our Promise Keeper is the source of our existence.

Testing and trials come
Along our paths of faith.
Do not give up;
Move in God's strength.
Remain a victor in the race.

ಆ ಈ

May 24
Hope, Strength, and Courage

"You are my lamp, O Lord; the Lord turns my darkness into light. With your help I can advance against a troop; with my God I can scale a wall." (2 Sam. 22:29–30)

Loving discipline balances the spiritual scale; lessons learned can be painful. O Lord, grant me joyful and trusting endurance that I may remain in the race and obtain Your victory! For You shine light in the chambers of my heart and scatter the darkness. Amen.

MEDITATION:
   The glory of the Lord transforms every bleak moment into a moment of twinkling hope, strength, and courage.

  O Come, Lord; quiet my heart.
  I need to hear Your voice today.
  Fear, grow silent; you can't stay…
  Jesus is speaking and I must obey.
  "Inquire Child, I AM the way;
  Remember My Word—and pray."

  Rejoice! Rejoice! a new song to sing…
  Faith bows to the heavenly King.
  "Be strong; be courageous
  For I hold your hand.
  You can do all things
  Through Me…you can!"

※ ※

May 25

The Condition of Our Hearts

"'[G]reat are your purposes and mighty are your deeds. Your eyes are open to all the ways of men; you reward everyone according to his conduct and as his deeds deserve.'" (Jer. 32:19)

 Lord Jesus, You counsel us with words of wisdom. You are God—full of holiness, justice, and truth. Teach us to be imitators of Your truth and help us grow in Your stature. Remind us, Lord, that every choice we make bears truth or consequences. Help us make choices based on Your standard of right living. May we receive Your grace to live our lives according to Your commands. Your commands safeguard our souls. Amen.

MEDITATION:
Jesus knows our weaknesses and the conditions of our hearts.

We are seen exactly the way we are, not the way we pretend to be or the way in which we hope to become. Our lives are wide open before a holy and just God, Who loves and accepts us just the way we are today. His great, unconditional love will never change. His grace will change us into His likeness. We must all be changed; but our God remains the same. His love cannot be expressed or understood—only accepted.

May 26

The Attentive and Watchful Eye of Almighty God

"He who sows wickedness reaps trouble, and the rod of his fury will be destroyed. A generous man will himself be blessed, for he shares his food with the poor." (Prov. 22:8–9)

Almighty God, we are so blessed to have Your written warnings, declaring we reap what we sow. Fill our hearts to overflowing with wisdom, truth, and compassion, Lord. Please bring forth the rains to cleanse our land, providing us with Living Water. Bless our land with godly people whose hearts are yielded to You. Give us strength to stand tall—and the grace when we need to stand alone. Amen.

MEDITATION:
Nothing escapes the attentive and watchful eye of Almighty God.

> We reap what we sow…
> Seeds are planted today.
> Seeds of doubt? Seeds of strife?
> Seeds of trusting always?

Doubt bears fear, and strife, discord,
But peace is sown for Him.

❦

May 27

He Will Renew Our Strength

"My heart is steadfast, O God; I will sing and make music with all my soul." (Ps. 108:1)

Father, true confidence is confidence that is unshakable… faith-filled confidence. I fix my thoughts on You and praise Your name. Make me a blessing to You today as Your Spirit moves through me. Amen.

MEDITATION:
As we confide in the Lord, trusting in Him completely, He will renew our strength.

In His Image

When people see me, Lord,
Will they see You through me?
When they take a closer look,
And peer into my soul…
Will they see a sinner
Who was called into the fold?
Send someone along my path,
Lord, by divine appointment,
That I may reach others
With the love of Jesus Christ.

❦

May 28

Trust

"O Lord Almighty, blessed is the man who trusts in you." (Ps. 84:12)

Help us in our struggles, O Lord, as we learn to lean on You.

Life's lessons teach us how to trust You. Strengthen us for Your service, and give us Your peace in the midst of upheaval. Confidently looking to You for wisdom and counsel, our hearts are filled with hope. And even though the trials hurt momentarily, You will exact good from them. Amen.

MEDITATION:
Trust has its own reward.

> When God's in every decision,
> There will be no remorse…
> As we learn to trust in Him
> And not in cultural choice.

May 29
God's Loving Gaze

"He who dwells in the shelter of the Most High will rest in the shadow of the Almighty." (Ps. 91:1)

All our internal systems that You created and fused together are dependent upon healthy and righteous living. Apart from You, we cannot even draw breath. For You, O Lord, know the brevity of our days. Teach us to appreciate today. Show us Your wondrous ways that we might live this day fully alive in You! Amen.

MEDITATION:
God's loving gaze steadies us; calmness is restored as we rest in the completeness of almighty God.

> God expresses loving encouragement to our hearts,
> otherwise we would fold under life's pressures.
> God's amazing grace is an oasis for our
> parched souls,
> a provision in our life journeys.

May 30

The Faithfulness of God

"I will say of the Lord, 'He is my refuge and my fortress, my God, in whom I trust.'" (Ps. 91:2)

Lord, our testimonies tell about Your holiness and faithfulness, your love to a thousand generations! Peace and joy come as we trust in God. Stir our souls to desire Your Word and counsel. Grant us the ability to serve You faithfully and joyously, proclaiming our God reins forever and ever! Amen.

MEDITATION:
We experience the faithfulness of God through many painful trials and expedient lessons.

> We move closer to God when all of our substitutes for security fail and God exposes the falsehood behind our allegiances. Only God can supply our every need, and He gives us true prosperity in our personal relationship with Him.
>
> He that engineered us knows us well; and He always has our best interests at heart. Thanks be to God for His Holy Spirit, Who indwells us, setting us free!

May 31

God Carries Us

"For he will command his angels concerning you to guard you in all your ways; they will lift you up in their hands, so that you will not strike your foot against a stone." (Ps. 91:11–12)

Lord, when we follow Your commandments, obeying Your voice and meditating on Your Word, then we have aligned ourselves to do Your will. Sovereign Lord, You are in control. Rule our hearts. Your ministering angels listen carefully to Your call as You dispatch directives on our behalf. Praise God for His mercy. Amen.

MEDITATION:
God carries us in His arms of everlasting love.

> God's Word is everlasting…
> He cannot fail.
> Will we meet the conditions
> That His promises unveil,
> Breathed by the Holy Spirit
> In a world groaning in travail?

∽§ ξ∾

June 1

Almighty God's Perfect Plan

"The law of the Lord is perfect, reviving the soul. The statutes of the Lord are trustworthy, making wise the simple." (Ps. 19:7)

Father, Your Word brings peace to our minds and is a medicine to our bodies, when we choose to apply it to everyday situations and circumstances, knowing that it is good. Your record of faithfulness and mercifulness, Your plan of salvation, Your ransom for mankind, Your wisdom—all this is given to those willing to hear and receive it. May we hear Your word. Amen.

MEDITATION:
Nothing can be added to Almighty God's perfect plan.

> God's Word refreshes our bodies and restores
> our souls to completeness and wholeness and
> harmony. Endurance, strength, and peace come
> from His merciful bounty. Our God is faithful
> to bear us up in His arms, to sustain us in fiery
> trials, to comfort us in our grief, and to rejoice
> with us in our victories—teaching us His
> ways. These are the benefits children of God
> receive.

∽§ ξ∾

June 2

Feed Daily on God's Word

"By them is your servant warned; in keeping them there is great reward." (Ps. 19:11)

Lord Jesus, freely we receive Your living Word and all of Your marvelous gifts. They're an anchor to our souls; our refreshment in the quake of battle. May our greatest desire be in loving You. Lord, You are worthy of having first place in our lives. We ask for Your mercy as You expose the "stuff" that fills the places of our hearts. Purge our souls that we may experience the manifestation of Your glorious power in our lives. Amen.

MEDITATION:

When we neglect to feed daily on God's Word and choose to feast our hearts on other things, our intake of inadequate nourishment manifests harmful side effects.

> He holds what is truly best:
> Perfect love to embrace.
> Diverted eyes cannot see
> Wondrous acts of mercy.

June 3

When the Heart is Unencumbered

"All the days of the oppressed are wretched, but the cheerful heart has a continual feast." (Prov. 15:15)

Lord, help us put into practice the wisdom and knowledge You have given us. The attitudes of our hearts determine our emotional responses. May we have "a continual feast" as we allow thoughts of Your goodness, Your power, and Your love to flow through our minds and hearts. Remind us to focus on Your Word. When our energies are nearing depletion, remind us that we have a well of Living Water that will replenish our souls. Let our hearts rejoice in fellowship with other believers. Amen.

MEDITATION:
Thoughts and creativity flow freely when the heart is unencumbered.

> God's signature lights the skies;
> Creation is displayed on high.
> Magnificent is the King!
> Treasure to hold,
> Riches untold—
> Our Father's offering.
> Cheery hearts are satisfied
> As they continually feast
> On the Word of their Guide.

ฉะ ฉะ

June 4

The Fullness of Life

"One man gives freely, yet gains even more; another withholds unduly, but comes to poverty." (Prov. 11:24)

Father, Your ways are different than ours. Teach us the meaning of Your instructive Word. Loosen our treasure; open our hands. For we could never outgive You. All the resources we have come from You. Thank You, precious Savior, for gifting Your people with ministerial abilities as You work mightily through them. We have been recipients of Your awesome grace, and we are stupefied by Your amazing love. Amen.

MEDITATION:
The Giver of Life emptied Himself to offer us the fullness of life.

> Millions of people gather at Your throne;
> Your grace brought them Home.
> Freely You gave, freely You give…
> Teaching foundational truths in love.

June 5

He Knows Our Steps

"He holds victory in store for the upright, he is a shield to those whose walk is blameless, for he guards the course of the just and protects the way of his faithful ones." (Prov. 2:7–8)

Father, You know our pathway to victory. Let us crucify pride. A life surrendered to Christ is a life well lived. May we be Christ-centered and Christ-dependent. You give us salvation. Wisdom and knowledge flow from Your throne. You crown us with success. We are esteemed as Your people. Amen.

MEDITATION:
He knows our steps.

> Safe in His presence, surrounded by His counsel, obedience becomes the driving force behind our chosen steps as we walk in faith.

◈ ◈

June 6

Touched by God's Love

"If you had responded to my rebuke, I would have poured out my heart to you and made my thoughts known to you." (Prov. 1:23)

Lord, I praise You for Your goodness and Your overwhelming love! Knowing that You desire to make Your thoughts known ushers us into the presence of Your intimate love. Gazing upon the beauty of Your holiness, the magnitude of Your love cannot be comprehended. Love exercises discipline. You cannot have one without the other. Amen.

MEDITATION:
We are profoundly touched by God's infinite love. It is known in the heart, experienced in the soul.

> His love continues from generation to generation. Rejoice! And know that God is faithful. He meets

us at our point of need, ministering healing to our wounded emotions and intellect. A new person emerges. Experiencing God's love, we are set free to proclaim His love and to rejoice in His righteousness.

June 7

Trust

"Trust in the Lord with all your heart and lean not on your own understanding; in all your ways acknowledge him, and he will make your paths straight." (Prov. 3:5–6)

Father, You know the scope of Your perfected plan for each one of us. You know the beginning…You know the end. We see things in short, imperfect frames. You have a glorious panoramic view, seeing us complete in You. Oftentimes we view life with distorted lenses. We so desperately need to trust You. Bring us to the place of surrendered trust, for You have chosen us to bring glory to Your name. Amen.

MEDITATION:
Trust remains even when there are no answers to the urgent questions of our hearts.

> Do we love You, Lord, when we cannot see our way?
> Do we remain loyal and faithful when emotions run astray?
> For You call us "Friend," and no greater Friend have we…
> Than our Heavenly Father, who walks closely.

June 8

Seedbed of the Heart

"As water reflects a face, so a man's heart reflects the man."
(Prov. 27:19)

Father, Your Truth is absolute. Who we really are buds deep inside us. We can have many pretenses and wear many masks, but according to Your time and place of exposure, others begin to know us by the attitudes of our hearts. "For out of the overflow of the heart the mouth speaks" (Matthew 12:34b). Heart lessons sharpen our senses, moving us closer to You. Amen.

MEDITATION:

The good seed that is dropped into the seedbed of the heart needs God's continual spiritual nourishment and protection.

> Heart seed germinates in God's nursery.
> Growing wings, thoughts take flight,
> Orbiting the recesses of our minds,
> A harbinger along our journey.

≈§ ε≈

June 9

Golden Apples

"He who walks with the wise grows wise, but a companion of fools suffers harm." (Prov. 13:20)

Lord, help us partnership with wisdom, blessing us with wisdom's friendship. "The fear of the Lord teaches a man wisdom" (Prov. 15:33a). Teach us this truth, O Lord, as we put our trust in You. Let us walk in faith, growing wise, as we learn to discern good and evil. Amen.

MEDITATION:

Mentors are gifts from God…friendship's golden apples.

> One day I'll stand before the King…
> Face to face I'll see His loveliness,

Friendship's golden apples of grace.

ಆ§ ફે&

June 10
Something Beautiful

"'I will repay you for the years the locusts have eaten—the great locust and the young locust, the other locusts and the locust swarm—my great army that I sent among you.'" (Joel 2:25)

Father, I praise You for Your promised Word—certainty among uncertainty. In thanksgiving and worship our hearts cry out to You in remembrance of Your promises. Blessings of renewal and restoration strengthen our weak frames from evil's injurious jabs. What was lost is gained. Endings give birth to beginnings. You honor Your Word. Lord, we give thanks for Your resurrection power in our lives. Amen.

MEDITATION:
Only God can make something beautiful out of a wasteland.

Resurrect our broken dreams,
Lord, into holy living scenes,
Filled with hope—visionary plans—
Abundant life lived through man.

ಆ§ ફે&

June 11
Everything We Have Comes from God

"But you have an anointing from the Holy One, and all of you know the truth." (1 John 2:20)

Holy God, You have given us an anointing. May we be found faithful in exercising our spiritual gifts. Open our eyes to behold You—to see You in all our daily tasks—the mundane and the magnificent. Forgive us when we have grieved Your Spirit and failed to abide in You. There are consequences to breaking fellowship with You. We become powerless as we attempt to move in our own strength; we are "strengthened with all power according to his glorious might" (Col.1:11a). As we plunge deeper into Your sweet fellowship, let our hearts reflect Your beauty and loving fragrance—hearts purified by Your refining touch. Amen.

MEDITATION:
Everything we have comes from God. Because of God's great love towards us, He has granted us His mercy and grace to succeed.

"Thank you" is a simple but endearing word. Our sincerity is shown as our kind deeds of appreciation are multiplied in the lives of others. We receive love so that we may give love, gifts and skills and talents given to glorify our Creator.

☙ ❧

June 12

Enabled by Almighty God

"The weapons we fight with are not the weapons of the world. On the contrary, they have divine power to demolish strongholds. We demolish arguments and every pretension that sets itself up and we take captive every thought to make it obedient to Christ." (2 Cor. 10:4–5)

Mighty God! Mighty Warrior! You have given us supernatural weapons: truth, righteousness (right standing with You), the gospel of peace (wholeness), salvation (redemption from the sins of the world), the Word, and the power of prayer. These mighty weapons wield Your strength and power, your "incomparably great power for us who believe" (Eph. 1:19a). Let us stand firm, putting our trust in You, Lord, as we "fight the good fight of the faith" (1 Tim. 6:12). In Jesus' name we pray. Amen.

MEDITATION:
Fully protected, fully shielded, and enabled by Almighty God,

we press on!

It is the goodness and wisdom of the Lord to put us into situations where we can receive divine training and practice—using the full armor of God—to withstand the enemy's assaults.

June 13

God's Language of Love

"Search me, O God, and know my heart; test me and know my anxious thoughts. See if there is any offensive way in me, and lead me in the way everlasting." (Ps. 139:23–24)

Father, Your searchlight is powerful, able to penetrate the deep recesses of my heart and innermost being. You expose and unfold my hidden faults and sins because of Your loving kindness toward me. Gently You come close to me with Your transforming touch of love, lifting me to higher ground and giving me manifold blessings. When I am tested, Lord, give me faith to cleave to You, trusting completely with unwavering faith, knowing that You are the Alpha and Omega. You alone are God and I am held safely in Your omnipotent arms of grace. Amen.

MEDITATION:
God's language of love is manifested in words and deeds of sacrificial giving.

Language of Love

Circle of Love, Eternal flame…
Breath of God, forever the same.
Holy Spirit, purge the earth…
Pointing man to Jesus' birth.
His body did not decay,
For He is risen! He is here always.
Open your heart…

Receive His Love…
Reign with Him above.
Do not make haste;
Stay the course of grace.
Abide in Him…
His goodness taste!

June 14

Hope

"Let the morning bring me word of your unfailing love, for I have put my trust in you. Show me the way I should go, for to you I lift up my soul." (Ps. 143:8)

I love You, Lord. My hope is in You and in "Your unfailing love." Abiding love is the grounds for happiness. Blessed is the believer whose trust is in You. Apart from You, we become open prey to the evil one and his world system. Darkness begs at our doors, seeking to devour us. Only You, Lord, have the power to infuse us with supernatural power and the spiritual nourishment that sustains our souls. Lord, in the morning when I awake, manifest Your amazing love in my heart and teach me to draw my strength from Your wellspring of life. Amen.

MEDITATION:
Our hope is in Christ alone.

God's love cannot fail.
Remembering His love
suffered at Calvary,
taking hold of the Promise
of eternal security,
God's resurrection power
Comforts me.

June 15

Walking in the Spirit

"For this reason, since the day we heard about you, we have not stopped praying for you and asking God to fill you with the knowledge of his will through all spiritual wisdom and understanding." (Col. 1:9)

Father, in order to know what Your will is for my life, first I need to know You. My prayer is to be filled with Your glorious wisdom and understanding, that I may obey Your precepts and understand Your purpose for my life…for Christ lives in me! Bring me to Your side, where obedience rules my flesh. Amen.

MEDITATION:
Walking in the Spirit makes great strides in His kingdom.

Letting go of what we think we know and
grasping truth awakens our senses into passion
that, once put into operation, creates a holy fire
that our bones cannot contain.

June 16

Truth

"Therefore do not be foolish, but understand what the Lord's will is. Do not get drunk on wine, which leads to debauchery. Instead, be filled with the Spirit." (Eph. 5:17–20)

Lord, Your Holy Spirit teaches us all things. It is Your will that we be filled with Your Spirit, experiencing joy in our lives, with thankful hearts. On our own we are helpless to live the Christian life; but we are given a Helper. Holy Spirit, flow through us. Amen.

MEDITATION:
To ignore God's truth is to have contempt for the written Word.

Without our eyes focused on Christ, we pursue life aimlessly.
Fulfillment is discovered in obedience to Him.
His desires become our desires, and the spark of His will ignites!
With God's approval and commission, all things are possible.

June 17

Submission to Christ

"You have laid down precepts that are to be fully obeyed. Oh, that my ways were steadfast in obeying your decrees!" (Ps. 119:4–5)

Lord, You know the way for my highest good. No matter how grievously my spirit bemoans or how confused I should feel, You will lead me along good and steady paths as I walk with You. Send Your ministering angels to uplift my soul. Amen.

MEDITATION:
Submission to Christ guards our emotions from having dominion over us.

We look straight ahead, eyes on Him…
We're washed in His blood…
Free from all sin.
Emotions grab hold,
Squeezing breath from inside,
Fighting dark opposition,
Our Warrior by our side.

June 18

We Are Comforted

"As a mother comforts her child, so will I comfort you; and you will be comforted over Jerusalem." (Isa. 66:13)

Father, Your love and grace comfort me, drawing me close. Faithfully, You gently embrace me with Your healing love. Mercifully, You respond to all our needs according to Your riches in Christ Jesus. At any given moment, we are free to approach Your throne of grace with the blessed assurance that the righteousness of Christ purifies us and places us in right standing with You. Amen.

MEDITATION:
God's unconditional love meets our needs, and we are comforted.

> Who would know the meaning of comfort
> If comfort were never given?
> Who would gain from our mistakes
> If lessons learned were not shared?

◈◈

June 19

Our Eternal Home, Our Heavenly Abode

"Open my eyes that I may see wonderful things in your law."
(Ps. 119:18)

Show me Your rich treasures in Your Word, Lord. Open my eyes to Truth. Guard me against distractions that I may meditate on Your Word. Lord, teach me how to prevail in prayer. Your Word is the key that unlocks wisdom. And godly wisdom creates a safe harbor for the children of God. Amen.

MEDITATION:
Our eternal home, our heavenly abode, is life with Him.

> He's preparing us now for greater
> adventure...our small steps beside His Kingly
> footprints. Only a foreshadow, inexpressible
> grace, calling us to holiness.

◈◈

June 20

Diligent unto the Harvest Time

"Sow your seed in the morning, and at evening let not your hands be idle, for you do not know which will succeed, whether this or that, or whether both will do equally well." (Eccl. 11:6)

Merciful Lord, You supply the seed to sow. From Your hand of grace we are given talents, gifts, and abilities. May we diligently perform the tasks given us, trusting You with the results. Open our hearts to Your Spirit's guidance. We ask that You, Lord, will be glorified and honored in all that we do. Amen.

MEDITATION:

As our Supplier gives seed to sow, may we be found diligent unto the harvest time.

> A myriad of talents and gifts are given to God's servants—friends of God. We are entrusted with His rich resources to reach the world with the knowledge of God's saving grace. We are observed in the workplace and at home, during good times and hard times. We are called to serve with excellence, thus mirroring the attitudes and attributes of people made in the image of Almighty God. His resources are too precious to waste. Let's give thanks, for we are a peculiar people, called to impact our world with Truth.

ଏଓ ଓଏ

June 21

A Land of Fruitfulness

"[H]ow blessed you will be, sowing your seed by every stream." (Isa. 32:20a)

Dear Lord, You give us fertile ground, even in the midst of calamity. You make things spring up with newness, brightness, and hopefulness. We are given many opportunities to grow and to serve. Will You find us willing to trust You with our lives, sowing seeds of obedience and faith? O God, help us to cast off useless garments of fear, despair, discouragement, and worry and to put on a garment of praise. Direct our paths, for You are our song of glory, our seed of promise. Amen.

MEDITATION:
God's triumphant call brings us into a land of fruitfulness.

>   Following is sometimes very hard to do, although
>   Knowing God is leading makes it easier to choose.
>   Don't give in to temptation's pleading word to stray...
>   Remember Who is in control, and just begin to pray.

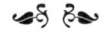

June 22

God's Faithfulness

"Yet I am always with you; you hold me by my right hand." (Ps. 73:23)

Father, I am comforted by Your presence, reassured by Your touch. Holding on to Your Word, I am embraced by Your wondrous and compassionate love. Even though there are times when my emotions cry out pain, I can find blessed rest in Your open arms of eternal love. Amen.

MEDITATION:
God's faithfulness reaches to the ends of the earth.

>   Together we are one.
>   My spirit soars
>   On Your wings of love.
>   I close my eyes...whisper a prayer...

So grateful, dear Father,
You're always here.
You will stay very close,
Guarding me with angelic host.

June 23

We Are Indebted to Him Forever

"He has delivered us from such a deadly peril, and he will deliver us. On him we have set our hope that he will continue to deliver us, as you help us by your prayers. Then many will give thanks on our behalf for the gracious favor granted us in answer to the prayers of many." (2 Cor. 1:10–11)

Precious and Merciful Savior, thank You for present-day miracles! Jehovah Rapha, God our Healer, only You, Lord, can snatch us from the jaws of death and completely restore us. You grant us our first breath and our last breath. I praise You, Lord, for gifts of mercy, comfort, and love. Quickly You come—quickly You hear our cries before an utterance can be made. It is You Who establishes intercessors on our behalf. Praise God for love that cannot be requited. Amen.

MEDITATION:
God is the only One Who can never be paid back. We are indebted to Him forever. He is our God Who gives deliberately and passionately, without persuasion. His goodness and mercy no one can measure…it has no end.

Thank You, Father, for each new day;
Ups and downs come, but will not stay.
Stronger we grow as roots dig deep down,
Drinking up rain through the dry, parched ground.
Remind us to drink from the Fountain of Life,
Ceasing from worry and abandoning all strife.
For You are our Keeper, King above all others…
Hell cannot prevail against the blood of our Brother. Amen.

June 24

When the Way is Unclear

"'If you have raced with men on foot and they have worn you out, how can you compete with horses? If you stumble in safe country, how will you manage in the thickets by the Jordan?'" (Jer. 12:5)

Lord God, prepare us to withstand those harsh seasonal whirlwinds, storms, and tempests that assail us. They will come…they will pass…and we will stand in the strength of our Lord. We have Your everlasting arms to embrace us. In every situation and circumstance we can enter Your presence, for You are El Shaddai, Almighty God. Teach us to draw our strength from You and to worship You in the midst of our enemies. Amen.

MEDITATION:
When the way is unclear and fear abounds, we can reach within and draw from the inner filling of God's Word that is deposited inside our hearts.

> When we grow weary and want to give up during good times, when everything is going well for us, how will we respond to tough times? When we cannot clearly see our way, will we give in to our emotions and run away from God's provision? What we do today determines tomorrow's successes. Our usefulness to Almighty God only requires the release of self into His open arms. He will make spiritual strides in our lives in season and out of season, when we are stretching and flexing spiritual muscles, and when we are resting in God's sovereignty.

June 25

God's Intervening Love

"Yet this I call to mind and therefore I have hope: Because of the Lord's great love we are not consumed, for his compassions never fail." (Lam. 3:21–22)

You never run out of dispensing mercy, compassion, and lovingkindness. You are our Redeemer—and into Your hands we offer up our sin-torn lives. Thank You for new life, bright beginnings, and new directions. For the sun's rays on cloudy days. For friends and memories. For new opportunities to grow in faith. Now may we shine with the light of Your countenance and truly live for You. Amen.

MEDITATION:
God's intervening love frees us from complete destruction.

> You short-circuit our pre-wired ways of destruction as You gently come in faithfulness and extraordinary love. Left to ourselves we'd wander into unfathomable darkness, but You, O God, of glorious Light, reach for us in love. Surrendering our earthly ways to kingdom living, we rise above the world's system. Not my way but Yours, O Lord. Not my way but Yours. Amen.

June 26

The Supreme Model of Friendship

"A man of many companions may come to ruin, but there is a friend who sticks close than a brother." (Prov. 18:24)

Jesus, You never grow weary of hearing our problems and seeing our misery. You invite us to cast all our anxieties upon You (1 Pet. 5:7). You are a friend that is trustworthy—unblemished and without sin—only interested in our highest good. The desire of Your heart is that we remain in close fellowship with You, becoming one in the Spirit. Thank You, Jesus, for Your saving love. Draw us closer into communion with You that we might experience the fullness of Your love that only is found in "a friend who sticks closer than a brother." Amen.

MEDITATION:
Fellowshipping with our Brother is the supreme model of friendship.

> We cannot give away the love of Christ to others if we have not received and experienced His love in our lives. Friendship with Christ teaches us how to love one another in purity, without expectations or demands as a precursor to friendship, accepting one another as we are. For only He knows what we are capable of becoming.

June 27

Praise is the Heart's Response

"So God created man in his own image, in the image of God he created him; male and female he created them." (Gen. 1:27)

Lord, You have made us in Your likeness! You, O God, have lifted us high, from dust to an eternal destination, forever changing us into the likeness of Your Son. Let us not resist Your masterful touch of perfection as we are being transformed into Your likeness. It is a skilled Surgeon's hands of mercy tenderly repairing and restoring our broken bodies of sinfulness into bodies of wholeness as we remain connected to You. For You desire us to glorify You with all of our being. To give You the respect and honor that is rightfully Yours. May our gaze steadily be fixed on You, O God, as we lift Your name high. You are our Banner faithfully going before us—our Banner of Victory. Amen.

MEDITATION:
God created His very best in man. Praise is the heart's response to the Master's handiwork.

Continuous praise flows from a thankful heart. Sung in eloquent silence deep within the soul is a melodious sound of contentment as we rest in the arms of God, ceasing to struggle, trusting in His sovereignty.

❧ ☙

June 28
His Awesome Miracles

"He performs wonders that cannot be fathomed, miracles that cannot be counted." (Job 9:10)

Yes, Father, I have seen Your miracles performed. How mighty and awesome You are, O God! Swiftly You come, bringing peace and comfort. Whether we lie in a bed of pain or are struck by disease, desolation, poverty, affliction, or mourning—You are there. You hold our hands and breathe tranquillity into our frames of dust. You summon the whirlwinds to be still. When the skies darken, O God, You flood our souls with light. Faith anchors our souls and blessings from Your hand satisfy our needy bodies. We are kept by Your compassionate and merciful love in all circumstances. Eagerly we take in the sustenance that You supply. Abba, Father, we bow to Your awesome presence, for in the night we discover that You are real. Your light illuminates our limited capacity to understand such amazing love. Freely You give; freely You come. Savior, keep us close to You. Amen.

MEDITATION:
God *is* still performing His awesome miracles, visiting us with His tremendous and merciful unconditional love.

Close your eyes and know that God is close.
It's when life's upside down
We must trust Him most!

Though we can't see Him with the eye,
His love is nestled deep inside.
For it is in trusting
We learn to run
Into our Father's arms
When difficulties come.
He will never reject our love,
No, never push us away...
For He is "a man of sorrows" (Isa. 53:3)
Welcoming us to stay.

June 29

Almighty God

"Exalt the Lord our God and worship at his footstool; he is holy."
(Ps. 99:5)

Lord, I praise Your holy name! You are worthy to receive all the praise that my soul can proclaim. My soul is filled with the gladness and joy of the Lord. Nothing can separate Your love from its dwelling place within my soul. I'm held captive by Your beauty, O Lord, and marvel at Your open hand of love. You are good, Lord, and I am satisfied by Your love. Amen.

MEDITATION:
We learn at the feet of Almighty God.

We come before Almighty God as needy children whose very lives are dependent on His parentage. We leave His feet revitalized and satisfied because our Father knows every need spoken and unspoken...only He can meet all our needs. His resources are as mysterious as they are countless, and we are awestruck by His majesty. Not time nor performance, position, education, or good deeds have any bearing on God's chosen manifestations of answered prayer in our lives. All that matters is our heart condition. God is most interested in a heart that is surrendered to His will—to His leadership, guidance, direction—and in children who are committed to Him as He lives and works through them.

✥ ✥

June 30

Victory

"Let us fix our eyes on Jesus, the author and perfecter of our faith, who for the joy set before him endured the cross, scorning its shame, and sat down at the right hand of the throne of God." (Heb. 12:2)

Scripture has given us many examples of heroes of faith. As children bearing Your name, will we too be found faithful? Will You find us standing tall after the howling winds of testing assail us? Is our strength small, O Lord? Are we prepared to suffer? Learning how to trust You, Lord, in our struggles, walking through them, we are strengthened by refining fire. We are comforted by Your Holy Spirit's touch. Our aching hearts are soothed with Your tender compassion. Lord, sufficient is Your grace and amazing is Your mercy! Triumphantly a new song is sung in the night. Our absolute hope in You blasts away the iceberg of uncertainties. You crown us with victory! We have joy in Your sight. Your grace is forevermore. Amen.

MEDITATION:
  Christ, the promise of victory!

  Whatever comes against me,
  You will bear the burden.
  Keep me in Your resting place,
  Above the tempest's fury.
  Meet me in my darkest night,
  Where we can be alone.
  Breathe on me, O Lord;
  Breathe life into my bones.
  Speak joy to my heart,

Lord; sing over me…
Calm the fears,
Calm the storm,
Carry me in Your arms.

July 1

His Covenant Love

"For this reason I kneel before the Father, from whom his whole family in heaven and on earth derives its name." (Eph. 3:14–15)

Amen! Father, it is true…Your resources have no end…every need we have is met in Christ Jesus because of Your vast love for us. Great are Your riches from Your omnipotent hand of glory. We draw our strength from You and are fit for spiritual battle. Abba, Father, You do for us what we are not able to do for ourselves. Mighty is our God and great are His works. Amen.

MEDITATION:
Strength flows from God filling our hearts with His covenant love.

Our hearts are filled with Divine love to fulfill
His plan and to go forward with the confidence
of God, accomplishing those tasks we are
called to trust Him with as He works through
us. For God has a special assignment for each
child of His. We are asked only to trust and
obey the Holy Spirit's prompting. God will take
care of the results. He is the Alpha and the
Omega. He is God!

July 2

Radically Changed

"Examine yourselves to see whether you are in the faith; test yourselves. Do you not realize that Christ Jesus is in you—unless of course, you fail the test? (2 Cor. 13:5)

Faithful Father, God of love, You discipline and instruct us in the way we should go. May we become imitators of our Lord. Draw us closer. Send the tests that we might be strengthened and that others will look at us and know we belong to You. We run into open arms of refuge and find Your peace embracing us. Amen.

MEDITATION:
Our thinking is radically changed when we come apart and commune with Almighty God.

> Commitment means that we hold fast to our faith, as we trust in God's sovereignty, even in the face of severe conflict and very trying circumstances. Are we controlled by the Holy Spirit or by our emotions? Do we base decisions on the appearance of good or on the promises of God? Partnering with Christ is the surest foundation now and throughout eternity.

July 3

Serve Him with Honor

"For the word of God is living and active. Sharper than any double-edged sword, it penetrates even to dividing soul and spirit, joints and marrow; it judges the thoughts and attitudes of the heart."
(Heb. 4:12)

Only You, Lord, can change us into people who are eager to obey and to do Your will, focusing on Your desires to be lived out in our lives. You know our stubborn and resistant hearts—our need for Your intervention. It is You, O God, who fulfills us with contentment and purpose. Reach down and rescue us from self-destruction. Freedom is in yielding to Your commands, giving us instruction that overflows with bounteous provision and protection. Anoint us Lord, with a new attitude. Amen.

MEDITATION:
Jesus redeemed our lives from the pit of destruction that we may serve Him with honor and glorify His name!

> Everything we do in Christ's name bears His signature.
> We are overtaken with praise!
> Who is this new person transformed in a moment of rebirth?
> Our hands willingly and diligently serve Him.
> Pray that we do not slacken in our commitment to be Christ's glorious Bride—through good times and tough times, during seasons of sowing and harvest, for His name's sake.

July 4

The Nearness of God

"'Turn to me and be saved, all you ends of the earth; for I am God, and there is no other.'" (Isa. 45:22)

Lord, we look to You for salvation and guidance. You created us to give You glory. Your purposes unfold for our lives. May Your Church remain vitally connected to You. When we are tempted to take the easy road and disobey Your voice, do whatever it takes to restore our intimacy with You. May our ears and hearts be open to Your gentle nudging of correction. Your way, O Lord, not our way. Amen.

MEDITATION:
The nearness of God quiets and satisfies our souls.

> Thoughts of Christ's faithfulness and nearness wash over me like a waterfall. I'm quickened with hopeful expectation. God's grace is at work.

July 5

God's Answers and Ways

"The Sovereign Lord is my strength; he makes my feet like the feet of a deer, he enables me to go on the heights." (Hab. 3:19a)

Our strength comes from You, Lord God—it is You who energizes our spirits and empowers us to overcome our enemies. Our hope rests in You. We are clothed with Your righteousness. Safely we are led and carried through life's rough spots. You, O Lord, make smooth the paths we trod. Lift us higher than our imaginations and expectations can fathom as we remain holding on to Your mighty hand of strength and power. Amen.

MEDITATION:
God steadies our steps, one step at a time.

> The first step is the most difficult step.
> We're unsure…filled with uncertainty,
> We haven't been this way before.
> But godly confidence comes as more steps are taken.
> Looking back, we marvel at the first step
> fading in the distance…
> Looking ahead we reach the summit.

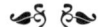

July 6

God's Divine Light

"But I trust in your unfailing love; my heart rejoices in your salvation." (Ps. 13:5)

Father, You have never failed me. Your mercy is a constant cloak of comfort that envelops my very soul. Your salvation brings a song of praise on my lips. Thank You for delivering me from darkness and bringing me into Your light. Teach me, O Lord, to trust in Your goodness. Amen.

MEDITATION:
Even in the darkest night God's divine light shines hope.

> He can be trusted to guide us today.
> God is in control, Captain of our soul!
> The water rises and storms prevail,
> But in His time He calms the gales.
> God is in control, Captain of our soul!
> When light breaks through the darkened skies,
> Peace is restored and turbulence subsides.
> Strengthened and wiser will we become,
> When we clasp His hand and believe
> God is in control, Captain of our soul!

◈

July 7

God's Spirit

"'Not by might, nor by power, but by my Spirit,' says the Lord Almighty." (Zech. 4:6b)

Lord, we triumph and succeed because of Your mercy and grace. When evil comes against us, You rescue us, Lord, and deliver us. What amazing grace! You, O God, breathe stillness and calmness into our souls in the midst of trials and persecutions. You send Your Spirit and we are refreshed and renewed. You suspend the world in Your powerful hands. We praise Your wondrous name, O Lord. Amen.

MEDITATION:
God's Spirit working through us is the reason for our success.

> All that we have comes from God.
> Choice is a gift and free will is divine.
> His Spirit has set us apart…
> His love embraces us.
> To God give the glory!

He blesses the work of our hands
for His highest good.

ઓફ ફે

July 8

Kingdom Power

"How good and pleasant it is when brothers live together in unity!" (Ps. 133:1)

Father, it is Your will that we assemble together to praise You and to fellowship in the spirit of love. We have been created with the need to fellowship. As we come together we are strengthened with ties that bind us together in love. There's a special anointing released as Your Holy Spirit moves within our innermost parts, every member of the Body serving one another in love. O Lord, we need one another…we need accountability…a check and balance to our spiritual walk. Let us come and "dwell together in unity!" Amen.

MEDITATION:
Kingdom harmony strikes a melodious cord in the heart of God.

Unity and harmony represent our love for
Christ.
For just as Christ has oneness with His Father,
we too are to have oneness with Christ,
displaying His love to one another.

ઓફ ફે

July 9

In the Simplicity of God's Love

"May my prayer be set before you like incense; may the lifting up of my hands be like the evening sacrifice." (Ps. 141:2)

Lord, may my prayer reach Your ears and touch Your heart. For You, O Lord, are holy, sovereign, and ruler of all. You pour

Your love inside me that I may pour out love. You give me peace in the night. When morning comes You are with me. You surround me with friends. I give You thanks and lift my voice to You in prayer. Father, thank You for Your presence and Your counsel of wisdom and encouragement. Amen.

MEDITATION:
In the simplicity of God's love, we find the meaning of life.

> With our hands lifted up to God, palms open to receive His desires, we acknowledge the fulfillment of every promise. Our worship and prayers are "as incense" as we seek His mind and face.

July 10

Hearts

"[A]nd if you spend yourselves in behalf of the hungry and satisfy the needs of the oppressed, then your light will rise in the darkness, and your night will become like the noonday." (Isa. 58:10)

Provision and protection are in Your principals and commands, O God. Words full of life impart wisdom and instruction to our weary minds. As we sow mercy, compassion, and kindness to one another, we also will reap these very things for our souls. In our time of need we reach out to touch lives and find fullness for our souls. Amen.

MEDITATION:
Christ touches hearts to meet needs.

> What I have to offer isn't from me;
> Christ is giving all that you see.
> Take and share with others in need,
> Freely giving His love generously.

July 11

The Watchful Eye of God

"The Lord is slow to anger and great in power; the Lord will not leave the guilty unpunished. His way is in the whirlwind and the storm, and clouds are the dust of his feet." (Nah. 1:3)

Lord, You are merciful, long-suffering, and just. As our perfect Father, You must discipline us. May we turn to You in confession and repentance to receive clean hearts, O God. Sovereign Ruler, have Your way in the tempest. Break our hearts that we might cry out to You in submission and reverence. You will meet every need we bring to You. Faithful and just is our God. Amen.

MEDITATION:
Nothing escapes the watchful eye of God.

>Tenderly He warns us to stay close by His side;
>Wandering sheep aren't safe away from their Guide.
>He's the wise Shepherd that directs our paths;
>His wise sheep know and obey His voice.
>God will discipline us to redirect our steps
>When we become weakened and transgress.
>For the Shepherd knows the dangers at hand…
>Lessons learned shape our minds to understand
>The importance of trusting His every command!

July 12

Swing Open the Gateway

"And we, who with unveiled faces all reflect the Lord's glory, are being transformed into his likeness with ever-increasing glory, which comes from the Lord, who is the Spirit." (2 Cor. 3:18)

O God…how awesome to know that we grow into Your likeness. Slowly, ever so gradually our character and personality take upon the traits of our Lord as Your Spirit moves within us.

Manifest the fruit of Your Spirit in our lives, so that others will see Christ in us. Open their eyes, O Lord, to see love in action. In Jesus' name. Amen.

MEDITATION:
Swing open the gateway to your heart, trusting God to fill it with His love.

We are not left without our Creator's eternal love and constant help. No experience is wasted with God in the center of our lives. He turns darkness into radiant light and sorrow into healing "oil of gladness"…in His time (Isa. 61:3b).

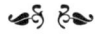

July 13

Hold On

"…[H]olding on to faith and a good conscience. Some have rejected these and so have shipwrecked their faith." (1 Tim. 1:19)

Father, You are teaching us to walk by faith. As faith is lived out, peace resides. When we stumble and yield to doubt, then anxiety and worry become unwelcome guests at our door, beggars longing to steal our joy. Teach us, Lord, to fellowship with Your Holy Spirit, leaning completely on faith, rejecting all intruders. Amen.

MEDITATION:
Hold on to God's pure and everlasting love.

> Holding on…holding on,
> Staying calm and holding on.
> Not knowing what tomorrow brings…
> Just knowing God's in everything.
> He cannot lie; His promises are sure.
> Resting in His arms, there is no stir.
> Doing my best, giving my all…
> Holding on…standing tall.

July 14

Our Keeper

"The Lord watches over you—the Lord is your shade at your right hand." (Ps. 121:5)

Lord, You are our protection. Because You hover over us, we are safe beneath "the shadow of your wings" (Ps. 17:8). The eyes of faith know what cannot be seen in the natural realm. And we know that You watch over Your children, faithful Father, yes—You hover over us. Blessed be Your name. Amen.

MEDITATION:
Our strength, our wholeness of mind, body, and soul—even our very breath drawn—come from the hand of God, our Keeper.

> I believe that God can use very ordinary people, filled with His Spirit, to accomplish manifold tasks, unimaginable to us, as witnesses of His glorious power. Our lives are being observed by others and read as open books. Will we be read as truth or fiction?

≈§ ≈

July 15

Manmade

"As for God, his way is perfect; the word of the Lord is flawless. He is a shield for all who take refuge in him." (Ps. 18:30)

You are my hiding place. I run to You and find refuge—peace and stillness. All things are in Your control—You bring good out of evil. Your light pierces the darkness. One look from You sends the enemy running. At Your command every living thing draws its breath and eats its food. We are dependent on You. Amen.

MEDITATION:
Worldly props are an illusion to a manmade world.

When life unravels like a pulled thread in a garment, trust God's faithful promises: He will never leave us or forsake us...He is with us always...Goodness and mercy will follow us all the days of our lives.

చ్రీ ఔ

July 16

God's Spirit Descends

"Suddenly there was such a violent earthquake that the foundations of the prison were shaken. At once all the prison doors flew open, and everybody's chains came loose." (Acts 16:26)

Only You, Father, can come on the scene so powerfully, mightily, and purposefully, acting in our stead and granting us deliverance. Deliverer...Advocate...Redeemer...Almighty God! Your timing is perfect. Your plan is our destiny. Amen.

MEDITATION:
God's Spirit descends, uprooting strongholds, freeing prisoners.

Suddenly

We never know when "suddenly" appears
To erase the pain and dry our tears.
God works with "sudden" surprise;
His right arm moves...
Joyous tears fall from our eyes.
It's enough to know
He is in control,
"Wooing" and interceding for souls.
His promises are faithful and true....
Yes, only God can do the impossible for you.
The Shepherd seeks lost sheep, 'tis true,
He can return, restore, and make brand new.
One day "suddenly" will come...
Your heart will leap...

Carried in God's arms
Will be lost sheep.

ৡ ৡ

July 17
No Room for Self

"Suddenly a sound like the blowing of a violent wind came from heaven and filled the whole house where they were sitting." (Acts 2:2)

Holy Spirit, come, refresh and renew discouraged hearts. Satisfy seeking souls thirsting for living water—expectant hearts longing to be filled with the righteousness of God. Set our hearts on fire with Your love, that we might touch others with the love and passion of Christ. Enlarge our hearts to receive the fullness of God's love. Amen.

MEDITATION:
When standing in God's presence, there is no room for self.

God's glory fills our hearts. Such goodness
makes us tremble as we worship and adore the
Holy One. His riches are imparted, giving us
the fullness of His Spirit. One day our tent will
fold, and with joy forevermore we will sing
praises at the throne of our King!

ৡ ৡ

July 18
The Hard Places of Persecution

"Have nothing to do with the fruitless deeds of darkness, but rather expose them." (Eph. 5:11)

Lord, may we not sway in our Christian walk. Give us wisdom and discernment to carefully choose our friends and the places we go and the things we say and do. Strengthen us for battle, lest we indulge the flesh and disobey the Spirit. Open the eyes of our heart and stir our passions for You. You are the fragrant offering of eternal life. Amen.

MEDITATION:
The enemy fled when Jesus said, "It is written" (Matt. 4:4a).

> We are fighting a supernatural battle. Our adversary's evil practices and vile ways are longstanding practices of deception. Scripture is our weapon to overcome and to dispel the confusion, flushing out the enemy with God's Truth. What we speak will build or destroy our faith. Speak Scripture. Believe Truth.

July 19

Counsel

"But you, man of God, flee from all this, and pursue righteousness, godliness, faith, love, endurance and gentleness." (1 Tim. 6:11)

Father, may we have singleness of heart, putting You in first place. Direct our steps to safe places as we move forward in our spiritual growth. Guide us with Your counsel. Teach us in our trials and hard places. May we be attentive to Your Word and live holy lives. In Your Name we pray. Amen.

MEDITATION:
God's counsel protects us.

> God's wisdom encircles us with loving protection, quickening our soul to pursue His righteous ways.

July 20

Our Circumstances

"But God, who comforts the downcast, comforted us by the coming of Titus." (2 Cor. 7:6)

Faithful Lord, countless times You have lifted us above the sinking sand of perilous circumstances. You have been a constant friend…our faithful companion…our helpmate. Thank You, Father, for the friends You have blessed us with and their loyal fellowship. Thank You for disbursing ministerial gifts and sending encouragers and comforters along our way who encouraged and comforted us by the ministry of Your Spirit. What a Savior we serve! Help us to be faithful in service. Amen.

MEDITATION:
God is in our circumstances.

> I cried to God, "This is not fair!"
> He listened compassionately;
> I knew He was there.
> Tenderly He comforted
> And stood by my side…
> Giving me His strength
> And the will to survive.
> Stronger I became each passing day,
> As He brought others along my way
> Who spoke a word or two
> Reminding me, "God loves you."
> Victory came and I held out my hand
> To help another hurting person stand.

July 21

God-Dependence

"Now to him who is able to do immeasurably more than all we ask or imagine, according to his power that is at work within us." (Eph. 3:20)

Father, You are able. Fill me with Your Spirit. Quicken my mind to Your truth so that my faith might not falter. Give me understanding of the vastness of Your great love. May I come before You in confident trust. Amen.

Meditation:
God-dependence begins on our knees.

> Talking to God in prayer
> Swallows up our daily cares.

⋞§ ₴⋟

July 22

Faith

"'See, he is puffed up; his desires are not upright—but the righteous will live by his faith.'" (Hab. 2:4)

Father, we need not concern ourselves with evildoers. Schemes perpetrated against us will be exposed. We are called to pray for our enemies, waiting on the Holy Spirit's power to rupture sin-filled hearts and allow healing. We are to live our lives in complete surrender to Your leading, moving forward in trust and confidence. Amen.

MEDITATION:
Faith is placing our lives in the hands of Almighty God.

> Believing God to meet our needs frees us to
> move forward in trust and confidence.

⋞§ ₴⋟

July 23

His Love Will Speak to You

"Know that the Lord is God. It is he who made us, and we are his; we are his people, the sheep of his pasture." (Ps. 100:3)

You are good, O Lord. We worship You in the holiness of Your name. In silence our hearts beat a love song that only Your Spirit can interpret. Receive joy, Lord, with the praise of Your people. Teach us to enter worship with hearts open wide. Let us adore You with sincere thanks and praise for Who You are. Amen.

MEDITATION:
Silence the thoughts that dart and dance; humble your self before the Savior's glance. For His love will speak to you.

In the stillness of this place,
I feel Your closeness,
I seek Your face.
And as You peer into my eyes,
This child is mesmerized.
For Your amazing love brings
A love song to sing:
"Be still and know that I am God" (Ps. 46:10a).
The time I spend with You
Is strength and sweet renewal.
In my Master's hand
Is a special, woven plan
That I need not worry about
Or have any fear or doubt.
On the *Promise of Hope* I stand.
In Christ I can! I can! I can!
There's a great cloud of witnesses above.
O let me proclaim my Savior's love.

July 24

Hearing and Obeying Blesses Our Paths

"I make known the end from the beginning, from ancient times, what is still to come. I say: My purpose will stand, and I will do all that I please." (Isa. 46:10)

Sovereign Father, what You speak, You will do. I love You, Lord. Fill this sinful world with righteous people whose hearts are laden with the spirit of generosity toward obedience and service. As we hear Your soft voice, let our responses be swift in application. From humble beginnings to splendid visions, may obedience in the small things be our standard of excellence for all things. Amen.

MEDITATION:
God's wondrous still voice directs our steps. Hearing and obeying blesses our paths with innumerable benefits.

> Like a mine waiting to be excavated
> Is a heart whose riches haven't been unearthed.
> Trust opens the heart to hear and obey,
> Unearthing hidden treasure to be shared.

July 25

Believing Faith

"Jesus answered, 'The work of God is this: to believe in the one he has sent.'" (John 6:29)

O God, we do not receive eternal life by doing good works. But because we have received eternal life, we cannot but help to do good works in Your name. You have made a way through the shedding of Christ's blood for the sin of mankind. Teach us, O God, to share the message of Your saving grace to a lost generation. Grant us zeal and boldness and eyes that are alert to divine opportunities in the ministry of reconciliation. Prepare hearts to receive Your unconditional love. Amen.

MEDITATION:
Believing faith is God's healing oil.

> Everything we have has been given to us.
> Gracious Lord, drop into our hungry hearts
> Your divine portion of spiritual sustenance.
> Increase our desire to serve, dividing our
> portion with those in need. Together our souls
> will be fattened.

July 26

If God Gave Us Everything

"Or do you show contempt for the riches of his kindness, tolerance and patience, not realizing that God's kindness leads you toward repentance?" (Rom. 2:4)

Lord, thank You for the riches of Your redemptive power. May our hearts burst forth with joyful praise in remembrance of Your costly grace! Forgive us, Lord, when we forget and become entangled in the tentacles of selfishness. Lead us in Your everlasting love, manifesting fruit in the kingdom of God. Amen.

MEDITATION:
If God gave us everything we "wanted," would we have our "needs" met?

> Searching for someone to fill a space only God
> can fill proved as futile as the excuses given.
> We are designed with a space reserved for
> God's holy residence.

July 27

The New Life That Fills Us

"To you, O Lord, I lift up my soul." (Ps. 25:1)

O Lord, all that I am I give to You. What is Your plan for my life, Lord? Where do You lead me? What is the next step to take? Your guidance will bring me to safe places. Take my fear and doubts, Lord, and teach me to trust in You; and then I will rest in Your arms, even in the midst of everyday challenges, knowing that Your love is wrapped securely around me. Make my life a blessing to You, O Lord! Amen.

MEDITATION:
The new life that fills us belongs to God.

> Give me a dream that I can achieve,

One filled with glory for my King.
Challenge my heart, soul, and mind;
Grant me courage to take the climb,
Unearthing God's treasure given me.

July 28

Forgiven

"See, I have engraved you on the palms of my hands; your walls are ever before me." (Isa. 49:16)

We are a part of You, Father, "engraved…on the palms of [Your holy] hands." And we have Your written Word upon our hearts. We are connected to You, loving Father, forevermore. You are everything we need. All our needs are met in You. Rule our hearts with Your love. Amen.

MEDITATION:
FORGIVEN.

Our Father's love is safe and secure.
Protected from harm, His love will endure.
No greater riches can fame or success bring
Than our Father's love healing sin's painful sting.

July 29

Our Father's Attentive Ears

"Everyone lies to his neighbor; their flattering lips speak with deception." (Ps. 12:2)

Father, guard my heart and mouth from speaking insincere words. Open my mouth to glorify Your name and to minister encouragement to others. Let Your Spirit quickly sear my conscience when I transgress against You. Give me grace today, Father, to listen as You speak. To love You is to obey You. Amen.

MEDITATION:
No word is left unheard by our Father's attentive ears.

> Our attentive, loving Father hears all our words.
> His ears are open to our complaints, cries, and praise.
> Nothing escapes our Father's merciful, loving gaze.

July 30

Spiritual Legacies

"For you have heard my vows, O God; you have given me the heritage of those who fear your name." (Ps. 61:5)

Father, our spiritual heritage is in Christ. We become light bearers fueled by Your Spirit and ignited by the grace of God. Help me pass the torch to my children. And may they pass the torch to future generations. Amen.

MEDITATION:
Spiritual legacies are passed from generation to generation.

> Solomon's Wisdom
>
> "Now all has been heard; here is the conclusion of the matter: Fear God and keep his commandments, for this is the whole duty of man" (Eccl. 12:13).

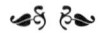

July 31

The Beginning of a Fruitful Life

"For I desire mercy, not sacrifice, and acknowledgment of God rather than burnt offerings." (Hos. 6:6)

Father, Your Word teaches us how to make good and right choices. You desire our alone time with You—a time of growing in intimacy—a time of learning to allow Your goodness to be made manifest in us. In Your written Word, You have given us mentors. Renew our minds and spirits, Lord, as we spend time with You. Our relationship with You is precious in Your sight. It cannot be bought, nor can we obtain the knowledge of our Lord without truly giving away ourselves to You. Take all I have, Father; I bow my knee to You. Amen.

MEDITATION:
A relationship with Christ is the beginning of a fruitful life; relationship first—everything else second.

> In God's perfect timing, the overflow of His riveting love smoothes the hard, encrusted spots on our hearts (evidenced by the attitude of our hearts), as we clamor for recognition and importance independent of God.

August 1

Weaned

"But I have stilled and quieted my soul; like a weaned child with its mother, like a weaned child is my soul within me." (Ps. 131:2)

Father, as we let go of our struggles, drawing closer to You, our hearts are quieted to the rhythm of Your heartbeat. "[L]ike a weaned child with its mother" we no longer are satisfied with milk, but with the meat of Your word. Amen.

MEDITATION:
We can be weaned from the world's view.

> When we align our thoughts to the mind of Christ, joy and peace pervade our souls, knowing that Christ is in control.

August 2

First Step

"Remember, O Lord, your great mercy and love, for they are from of old." (Ps. 25:6)

"The earth is the Lord's, and everything in it, the world, and all who live in it" (Ps. 24:1). I surrender to You, Lord, Your rightful place as Lord of my life. Receive my surrendered spirit, and touch my life with Your mercy and the fullness of Your design and purpose, as You live through me. Amen.

MEDITATION:
God is patiently waiting for us to take our important first step into His open arms.

"Things" appear important
(Far from our reach)...
Grabbing our attention
And eager to compete...
Voices attempt to override
Gentle callings of God's will.
While God is patiently waiting
For us to step into His arms.

August 3

Acceptance

"For the Lord will not reject his people; he will never forsake his inheritance." (Ps. 94:14)

Your loving arms are outstretched toward me. You take me in, O Lord, and cover me with Your Presence. In the fullness of Your love is sufficient strength and grace to meet my daily needs. Receive honor, Lord, with lips of praise. Purify my heart by the Refiner's fire. Your discipline is good for me. It teaches me to depend on You. Soften my heart that I might learn spiritual lessons quickly, growing up in the knowledge of My Redeemer.

Father, grant me the mind of Christ that I might become all that You desire. And lead me on a path that will continually glorify You. Make my life count for You! Amen.

MEDITATION:
Acceptance is God's answer to the world's rejection.

The treatment we receive from God is honorable and respectable. We are kings and princesses in His kingdom. Our Creator never pushes away His creation. Patiently He stands at our heart's door and knocks. A Holy God meets us in our worst condition. We choose whether to believe in Him and receive eternal blessing or to reject Him and receive eternal damnation. If we should foolishly decide to spurn God's counsel and live in rebellion, we can never blame God for the consequences. God's will is that we all come humbly before Him and live with Him forever. Christ's rejection and sacrificial death made a way for our acceptance for eternity with God.

◈ ◈

August 4

Radiant Smile

"The Lord is good to those whose hope is in him, to the one who seeks him." (Lam. 3:25)

Blessed Redeemer, You are good. Your thoughts toward us never diminish. Your heart of love flows through us. You revitalize our weary souls. Faithful Lord, thank You for Your spirit of joy and peace. Amen.

MEDITATION:
The presence of God warms the heart's dank corner.

God is the living hope in our hearts.

His love is beyond our understanding,
warming our Hearts with His presence.

***

August 5

Our Cornerstone

"In him the whole building is joined together and rises to become a holy temple in the Lord." (Eph. 2:21)

Father, what a glorious foundation we have. You have sent thousands upon thousands before us, faithfully holding a scepter of truth to pass on. You are able to make us stable, secure, and firm in a world filled with violence, confusion, and greed. Father, by grace we remain strong to finish what You have begun in our hearts. Amen.

MEDITATION:
Our foundation is not firm without Jesus Christ, our Cornerstone.

"And in him you too are being built together to become a dwelling in which God lives by his Spirit" (Eph. 2:22).

***

August 6

Faith Leads the Procession

"In him and through faith in him we may approach God with freedom and confidence." (Eph. 3:12)

Reign in our hearts, Lord Jesus, and free us from self. Flow a mighty river of salvation that we might live life fully. Restore our hearts to fully depend upon Your goodness and mercy. Amen.

MEDITATION:
Faith leads the procession of the army of God!

Child take flight…

Spread your wings…
Close beside you I soar!
While searching and trusting
And conquering new heights,
Look to Me, allowing
faith to quiet fear's roar!

୶ଚ ଚ୬

August 7

Eyes Focused on Truth

"The Lord is my light and my salvation—whom shall I fear? The Lord is the stronghold of my life—of whom shall I be afraid?" (Ps. 27:1)

Lord, as a tender shepherd watches over his sheep, You care for me. As I learn trust and obedience, replace fear and doubt with faith. My soul is fattened and satisfied by Your tender care. Amen.

MEDITATION:
The strain of worry is removed when eyes are focused on the Truth.

The application of truth overrides worry.
We cannot worry and trust God at the same time.

୶ଚ ଚ୬

August 8

Eternal Gain

"So Solomon built the temple and completed it." (1 Kings 6:14)

Jesus, give us the strength to remain committed to our tasks and to walk in truth. Temptation tries to pulls us down into an abyss of discontentment and confusion. O Lord, steady our weakened frames. Quicken our weary spirits so that we may complete the work at hand. Amen.

MEDITATION:
Eternal gain is in every Christ-centered deed.

> Holy Spirit, hover over us
> With Your gentle blowing wind...
> Mysteriously moving us along a path
> Marked by empowerment within.
>
> What You have begun in us,
> Complete in You it will be...
> Mercy touches a willing soul
> For the entire world to see.

August 9

Echoes of Love

"Do not gloat me, my enemy! Though I have fallen, I will rise. Though I sit in darkness, the Lord will be my light." (Mic. 7:8)

Father, You are great within me! I will rejoice in Your salvation. O lifter of my head, benefactor of grace, my own fears assault me, but remembrance of You invokes courage to persevere through the night, expecting Your glorious light to shine hope in the stronghold of battle. Our gallant and faithful warrior, merciful intercessor, defends my cause and vindicates me! Amen.

MEDITATION:
Rushing winds of God strum the quaking reeds into echoes of love.

> We rejoice because God is our liberating love song.
> We need not dwell on "if only." Today is a day of possibilities.

August 10

The Real Person Inside

"In everything I did, I showed you that by this kind of hard work we must help the weak, remembering the words the Lord Jesus himself said: 'It is more blessed to give than to receive.'" (Acts 20:35)

Father, we proclaim our love for You by loving one another. May we allow our tears to flow freely, comforting one another in love. Lord, may we be devoted in fellowship, strengthening our bonds of friendship. Amen.

MEDITATION:
Transparency allows the real person inside to be seen.

Open the window to my heart,
Bidding yesterday's hurts to be set free.
Today is a gift…a brand new start…
O heart, awaken! God's promises are for thee!

August 11

Honored

"Whoever serves me must follow me; and where I am, my servant also will be. My Father will honor the one who serves me." (John 12:26)

Give us Your grace and strength, O Lord, to never wink at sin. When we grow weary, remind us to take refreshment from the Vine. Lord, grant us steadfast courage and discipline to joyfully serve our King with due honor. We adore You, our glorious King! May You find us committed to following You all the days of our lives, as we draw our breath and might from You. Amen.

MEDITATION:
The highest reward of a servant is to be honored.

"Strength be the virtue for those who carry burdens and show not the strain but the spirit."

—Don Gunning

August 12

Sweet Communion

"For in him you have been enriched in every way—in all your speaking and in all your knowledge." (1 Cor. 1:5)

Father, how humbling it is to acknowledge that we are imperfect, blemished people whose faith rests completely in Your power. May we acknowledge our shortcomings and securely place our faith in Your hands. Our confidence is in You, O God, and from You we receive gladness of heart and tranquility. We are empowered by the Spirit, our divine teacher, to discern truth from falsehood. Closer to You, Lord, we come. Amen.

MEDITATION:

In sweet communion with our Lord, divine assignments are commissioned with power, purpose, and completion.

> Wisdom acknowledges the plan of God and
> faith executes its divine purpose. A completed
> mission is successful because our confidence
> and trust rests in our Commander whose orders
> we swiftly carry out.

August 13

All Things are Possible

"Solomon son of David established himself firmly over his kingdom, for the Lord his God was with him and made him exceedingly great." (2 Chron. 1:1)

Lord, You make us great. For all Your promises are "Amen." Whatever successes we have are because You have put Your hand upon us and made us prosper in Your kingdom. Amen.

MEDITATION:

With the hand of God resting upon us, all things are possible.

Above the trees, puffy clouds were drifting in the picturesque skies
As I methodically imagined the outcome of a dream to be realized.
My thoughts were gently interrupted by a still small voice inside,
"Are you willing to do what I have planned? I will guide."
The vision loomed before me and excitedly I thought,
How can this be? Then I remembered the comforting truth:
"All things are possible" with Thee.

❧ ☙

August 14

Inquire of the Lord

"He did evil because he had not set his heart on seeking the Lord."
(2 Chron. 12:14)

Lord, what a sharp contrast between obedient actions and disobedient actions. Our lives can be fully and joyfully lived as we set our hearts on Your desires, or we can be ensnared with evil because we set our hearts on those things that have taken Your place. We need Your wisdom and counsel, Lord, that we might fulfill our God-given potential. Amen.

MEDITATION:
To achieve our God-given destiny, we must inquire of the Lord.

Lord, I bend my knee to You,
Seeking Your wisdom in all that I do.
When I rise from bent knee,
May I obey You, Lord, faithfully.

❧ ☙

August 15

The Lord, Our Maker

"In His hand is the life of every creature and the breath of all mankind." (Job 12:10)

Lord, I place my confidence in You. You are my hope and my salvation. You have rescued me from the damnation of sin. Sovereign Lord and Ruler of all, lead me along paths of holiness and grant me perseverance and endurance, for Your name's sake. Pure and costly is Christ's shed blood for the sin of the world. I belong to You, O Lord. Shape my life into an instrument of service and honor unto You. Amen.

MEDITATION:
Honor and respect belong to the Lord, our Maker.

> Precious seed is oftentimes crushed in times of willful disobedience and resurrected by God's merciful forgiveness. Lessons learned teach many untold others to walk in His steps and love thy brothers.

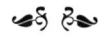

August 16

Purified by Fire

"Create in me a pure heart, O God, and renew a steadfast spirit within me." (Ps. 51:10)

O God, purify my heart. Grant me a strong, prevailing spirit that isn't tossed to and fro with the winds of change. And a heart after Your own heart. May my desires be Your desires, reflecting the attitude of Christ. Complete in me what You have begun, giving me sufficient courage to stay on course and grow in faith. I need Your help, O God. Grant me strength and a steadfast spirit. Amen.

MEDITATION:
Cleansed hearts are purified by fire.

The Refiner's fire is a melting pot of love.
The refining process cleanses hearts,
melting them into Christ-likeness.

ॐ ॐ

August 17

When We Run Ahead

"But they soon forgot what he had done and did not wait for his counsel." (Ps. 106:13)

Your timing, Lord, is perfect. Develop our characters to reflect the beauty and wonder created in Your own Son's image. Just as an undeveloped photo needs processing, we, who are made in Your image, need processing through the gentle sieving of the Holy Spirit. As we grow in the stature of Your precious Son, people will clearly see Jesus Christ in us. Lord, have Your perfect way in our lives. Amen.

MEDITATION:
When we run ahead of God, we miss blessings.

> If ever I forget
> And choose to run ahead,
> Where blessing once was,
> Disappointment will come instead.
> Taking one day at a time,
> Lord, and calling out to You
> Gives me Your blessed assurance
> That You're in all I say and do!

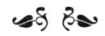

ॐ ॐ

August 18

Our Father

"As the mountains surround Jerusalem, so the Lord surrounds His people both now and forevermore." (Ps. 125:2)

Lord, You are our safe place. We run to You for protection, restoration, and rest. In You, Lord, we are strengthened and changed from glory to glory. Power and might come from You. You clothe us with Your Spirit. You are our lifeline of hope and joy on earth and for all eternity. Amen.

MEDITATION:
Our Father is unchangeable, immovable, secure, and steadfast in love.

> The Holy Spirit teaches us the deep truths of
> God, and we choose to rest in the security of
> His provision or to fall apart believing the lies
> of the enemy.

August 19

A Heart Attitude

"For nothing is impossible with God." (Luke 1:37)

Dear Lord, all things are possible. Stir the faith within my soul as I stand in the gap and pray, touching the hem of Your garment with thanksgiving and praise. Jesus, pray for me. Intercede on my behalf. You are my righteousness. You fulfill all Your promises. Those who trust in You are robed in garments of strength and joy. Amen.

MEDITATION:
Speak to impossibility with a heart attitude of possibility.

> Doubt robs; trust gives.
> Joy stealers feast on negativity.
> Satisfied and fattened souls
> Feast on God's ability.

August 20
Eternal Springs of Living Water

"This is the bread that came down from heaven. Your forefathers ate manna and died, but he who feeds on this bread will live forever." (John 6:58)

Father, thank You for leaving the riches of Your heavenly kingdom and becoming poor on earth that we might become rich in the eternal love of Christ. You emptied Yourself on the Cross, opening a pathway for us to receive the fullness of Christ. May we receive this bread and live forever. Amen.

MEDITATION:
Eternal springs of Living Water flow through the children of God.

> Bubbling brooks wash over the stones, just as
> God's Spirit washes over living stones—
> children of God—made in the image of the
> chief Cornerstone, Jesus Christ.

August 21
Our Inward Condition

"Never be lacking in zeal, but keep your spiritual fervor, serving the Lord." (Rom. 12:11)

Holy Spirit, set my heart ablaze with the Father's love. May Your love triumph in my circumstances. Shine, Holy Spirit, shine in my heart today. Guide my steps into His holiness, teaching me His precepts. May the Bride of Christ reflect the beauty of the Lord and be adorned with ornaments—the blessings of God. For God's riches are better than any thing this world has to offer. Amen.

MEDITATION:
Our inward condition is always displayed outwardly.

Nothing is hidden from God's tender look…
Closely he peers inside our deepest hurt.
His heart is touched with our grief…
A "man of sorrows" (Isa. 53:3)
He brings comfort and relief.
Even in this condition,
Serving God can overcome
All of life's trials and sorrows,
As we trust in God's Son.

୶ई ३॰

August 22

Growing Love

"May the Lord direct your hearts into God's love and Christ's perseverance." (2 Thess. 3:5)

Father, reveal to us Your faithful and steadfast love—love that called for the costly sacrifice of Your Son's blood to be poured out for the redemption of mankind. O what perfect love covers our sins, crowning us with everlasting life. Guard our hearts, as we wait for Your return. Amen.

MEDITATION:
Growing love cannot wallow in failure or regrets.

To leave the past behind
Calls for a future hope:
A destiny, a dream or two;
God's promises are for You!

୶ई ३॰

August 23

Speak the Word

"I appeal to you for my son Onesimus, who became my son while I was in chains." (Philem. 10)

Father, what an awesome privilege and honor to be a spiritual parent. Teach us how to disciple and mentor Your precious babes in Christ. We have been charged—commissioned to share the gospel with the lost. Empower us with boldness to snatch those that are perishing from the fire, and let us be an example of Your love in word, thought, and deed. In Christ's name we pray. Amen.

MEDITATION:
Pray for mouthpieces to speak the Word and for stars to shine in the darkness.

> God's omniscient transforming power changes "our way" into "His way."
> Lifted to higher ground, we know the many benefits of salvation.
> We are responsible and accountable for all that the Master has taught us.
> By His Spirit, we have been enriched, enlightened, and strengthened.
> We will never be the same, nor will we be able to return to the old.
> Having been transformed, we turn to God; having forsaken our
> former courses, we belong to Him, Who has set us apart for His glory.

 ❧ ☙

August 24

Our Faithful Companion and Guide

"I myself said, 'How gladly would I treat you like sons and give you a desirable land, the most beautiful inheritance of any nation.' I thought you would call me 'Father' and not turn away from following me." (Jer. 3:19)

Father, we are weak and needy and have lost our way. We have broken covenant relationship with You. Hear our prayer, O Lord, and forgive us. Our tears of sorrow overwhelm us. Revive us, lest we remain overwhelmed. Comfort us, drawing us close to Your bosom, dear Lord. We return to You. Following in Your steps, we are revived. Amen.

MEDITATION:

God is our faithful companion and guide, full of tender mercy and compassion.

His Hand Holding Mine

I clasped His hand;
It was so strong.
With tears I kissed
The One I've wronged.
His hand is truth;
His hand is life.
The sinless One brings peace
Where there's strife.
His hand holds promise;
His hand guides the way.
Forever at His side
Will be His bride.

ಆ§ ೭*

August 25

No Higher Honor

"He said: 'O Lord, God of Israel, there is no God like you in heaven or on earth—you who keep your covenant of love with your servants who continue wholeheartedly in your way.'" (2 Chron. 6:14)

We love You, Lord. We kneel before Your throne of mercy. Receive our worship. When words cannot express what's on our hearts, listen to our hearts. Receive joy, our Lord, as we sing praises to You. Amen.

MEDITATION:

The Lord's covenant is firmly established.

We can choose to be covenant keepers or cov-

enant breakers.
God has empowered us to make the right choice. Free will allows us to make the choice.

August 26

The All-wise Arms

"Even to your old age and gray hairs I am he, I am he who will sustain you. I have made you and I will carry you; I will sustain you and I will rescue you." (Isa. 46:4)

You wrap Your arms around us. You will carry, sustain, and rescue us. Thank You, precious Lord, for meeting our needs. We humbly acknowledge our desperate neediness and dependency upon You. May we cut the clinging apron strings attached to other things and reach out for Your guidance and direction. Our days are counted…You appoint our seasons and order our steps. Life forevermore is Your gift of salvation. Amen.

MEDITATION:
Recline in the all-wise arms of a loving God.

God's abundant grace gently teaches us principles of right living, protecting us from perilous evil at the crossroads of right and wrong choices. Choose to learn from Him and know the principles of godly living, reaping eternal value.

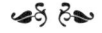

August 27

Confidence

"I will wait for you, O Lord; you will answer, O Lord my God." (Ps. 38:15)

O Lord, You are my confidence. Man disappoints…but You,

Lord, are just and true. You hear our prayers. Answer our prayers according to Your wisdom and loving-kindness, O Lord. We praise Your name and meditate on Your Word. Amen.

MEDITATION:
Faith in God exudes godly confidence.

> When the object of your love is faithful and true,
> Desiring only to give what is best for you,
> Hope and love are rekindled again.

August 28

God's Love Reaches Us

"Do everything in love." (1 Cor. 16:14)

Dear God, let our love be sincere toward one another. Others need to see love in action. We are testimonies of Your grace and abundant blessings. The Holy Spirit lives in our bodies, a tabernacle of Your creation. May our responses to the many struggles and joys of living be a display of Your great power and grace flowing through us. In all that we do may we reflect Your love. Amen.

MEDITATION:
God's love through us touches the world.

> Love upsets the plans of evil,
> With power so divine…
> Far-reaching it can conquer foes,
> When Christ is first in line.

August 29

Love and Honor

"However, each one of you also must love his wife as he loves himself, and the wife must respect her husband." (Eph. 5:33)

Heavenly Father, let us be men and women of excellence, called by divine grace as encouragers and comforters. May our speech be uplifting. Lord, teach us to value our uniqueness, growing up in our full potential in Christ. Amen.

MEDITATION:
Love and honor make a great twosome for marriage.

> I mirror to you what I would like to receive...
> Kindness and mercy remedies most needs.
> Memories are multiplied by caring deeds...
> Love is embraced in small thoughtful things.

ఇ ఏ

August 30

Divine Apparel

"Then the Spirit of the Lord came upon Gideon." (Judg. 6:34a)

Holy Spirit, we welcome Your immersed love. Clothe us with holiness. Enable us to go forth in strength, armed for service. We yield to Your control, giving You thanks for Your sweet abiding fellowship. Amen.

MEDITATION:
We are covered with divine apparel.

> "Rather, clothe yourselves with the Lord Jesus
> Christ, and do not think about how to gratify
> the desires of the sinful nature" (Rom. 13:14).

ఇ ఏ

August 31

Integrity

"Do not show partiality in judging; hear both small and great alike. Do not be afraid of any man, for judgment belongs to God. Bring me any case too hard for you, and I will hear it." (Deut. 1:17)

Father, may we be people of integrity. Swiftly convict us when we attempt to justify wrongdoing with deceptive pride. When man is against us, O God, remind us that You are for us. You are the final judge—and You have the last word. Give us wisdom for every decision, and strengthen us in the face of opposition. Our help and vindication come from You. Let us seek Your face before we receive any counsel from godly people. For You, dear God, are truth and justice. Amen.

MEDITATION:
Integrity is looking in the mirror and seeing God's reflection.

> Wisdom drinks from a fountain of truth.
> Fools pass by and thirst.

September 1

No Birth Order in Christ's Family

"There is neither Jew nor Greek, slave nor free, male nor female, for you are all one in Christ Jesus." (Gal. 3:28)

Thank You, Father, for breaking down every wall and overcoming every opposition. There are no divisions or barriers that can prevent Your love from reaching us. Perfect love binds us together in unity. Perfect love has no favorites. Amen.

MEDITATION:
There is no birth order in Christ's family.

> Loving Father, Highest Priest,
> Good and faithful, God of peace,
> We are created by design:
> Our Master's touch,
> Tender and kind.
> He who walked upon this earth
> Powerfully indwells us with rebirth—
> Those who are last shall be first.

September 2

Arrogance

"For rebellion is like the sin of divination, and arrogance like the evil of idolatry. Because you have rejected the word of the Lord, he has rejected you as king." (1 Sam. 15:23)

Lord, while in Your glorious custody, we are nurtured and directed—prepared to go at Your command. But what evil and disaster awaits those who languish in rebellion, wearing the deceptive mask of arrogance. When light is squelched, how very dark the darkness becomes. Amen.

MEDITATION:
We engage in the deceptive dance of idolatry whenever we partner with arrogance.

> Lord, begin Your restorative work
> that I might dance before You in worship.

September 3

Great Gain

"Godly sorrow brings repentance that leads to salvation and leaves no regret, but worldly sorrow brings death." (2 Cor. 7:10)

Dear Father, as we yield our broken clay vessels to Your will, reparation begins. Use all of our painful experiences producing in us a harvest of goodness, for Your Name's sake. And when we recall our past mistakes and pain, let us remember the wondrous ways You have worked good in our lives from the ruinous heaps of destruction. With thankful and worshipful hearts, we entreat Your glorious presence with joy. Amen.

MEDITATION:
God can take our pain and yield great gain.

> What profit do pain and hard lessons bring
> When eyes are red and the truth stings?

The tough places teach us many things.
Compassion settles around the wound…
God's perspective gives us wisdom, too,
As we endure and grow in grace.

September 4

Our Good and Loving Father

"[A]lways give thanks to God the Father for everything, in the name of our Lord Jesus Christ." (Eph. 5:20)

Glorious Lord, as we learn to trust You completely, with our lives consecrated to Your divine authority and care, then we will find ourselves praising You with overflowing thanksgiving for all things. For when we no longer hold on to unbelief in what You are capable of doing in our lives, then, we will know in complete trust that You are always working toward our very best interest. Instead of doubts and fears as lurking shadows of intense uneasiness, renewed belief in Your sovereignty and wisdom will emerge as a fresh wind. Father, forgive us for breaking Your heart with our worry that somehow You wouldn't provide for all of our needs, all the time. With gratefulness and praise, receive our open hearts of repentant prayer and joyful thanksgiving! Amen.

MEDITATION:
Our good and loving Father holds us gently and securely in the palm of His all-knowing, all-powerful, all-wise hand.

Jesus is moving…
His Spirit covers thee.
Rejoice in God's power;
Rejoice in God's peace.
Forever He is with us;
Forever we are free.
Praise the Almighty!
Praise God we're free!

September 5

Aim High Above

"Since, then, you have been raised with Christ, set your hearts on things above, where Christ is seated at the right hand of God." (Col. 3:1)

Thank You, blessed Jesus, for new life! Grant us the courage to walk where You lead. As sons and daughters, may we remain devoted to You. Give us Your perspective, Your mindset, and enlarge our hearts to receive the full measure of Your love. Help us to understand that the first relationship we need to cultivate is an intimate relationship with You, for this is the true foundation that all other relationships are built upon. Help us to grow up in the reflection and beauty of Your love. Amen.

MEDITATION:
Aim high—look to the heavens.

Earthly riches will soon disappear.
Heavenly treasure is everlasting.
Sow earthly seed for eternal reaping.

September 6

Established

"'I will be a Father to you, and you will be my sons and daughters,' says the Lord Almighty." (2 Cor. 6:18)

Wondrous Father! What an incredible heritage You have given Your children…roots in Christ Jesus, the Planter of our souls. Father, the mantle over us is a glorious covering protecting the soul. Thank You for the garment of salvation. The family tree we belong to is grounded upon a solid and sure foundation forevermore. May we bring joy and pleasure to You, as we imitate the love of Christ. Amen.

MEDITATION:
Fierce winds cannot topple over established saints.

Roots dug deep in Christ
Withstand life's storms.
I trust You, Loving Father;
You will care for me.

ॐ ॐ

September 7

The Bloodline of Jesus Christ

"I will be his father, and he will be my son." (2 Sam. 7:14a)

Dear Father, David became Your anointed son, and You desire that we become Your anointed children. Because of Your lovingkindness and mercy, we can enter Your court and become Your adopted children. Your Word says that we become Your children as we receive You into our lives (John 1:12). And as children of the King, we have been granted ministerial gifts—gifts to be lavishly released and ministered to the body of Christ. May we be faithful in service! What an incredible privilege to be in relationship with You and to be called sons and daughters. You are faithful, even when we shrink back from fellowship and veer from the path. Forgive us, dear Lord. Guard our hearts from anything or anyone that would pull us away from a growing intimacy with You. Amen.

MEDITATION:
Jesus Christ is our lifeline to eternal life.

> Give me a victorious heart of prayer, O God:
> Place the weapon of prevailing prayer in my hand.
> With Your Word full of life, I'll succeed, dear God,
> Resting in Your arms when I've done all that I can.
> Though opposition may war against Your plan
> And a snare has been laid before me,
> By Your Spirit I'll stand; by grace I can,
> As Your Spirit tenderly hovers over me.

ॐ ॐ

September 8

God's Gentle Instruction

"'Turn to me and be saved, all you ends of the earth; for I am God, and there is no other.'" (Isa. 45:22)

Dear God, stir our hearts to seek Your face and to fall in love with Jesus. May we run into His waiting arms, outstretched arms—arms that were outstretched on a tree for all of humanity. When we stand before You, how will we answer for our unbelief? Today let us receive Your words, "Turn to me and be saved." We come before You, Lord…we come. Amen.

MEDITATION:
God's gentle instruction comes lovingly sent with promises and warnings.

> Worldly promises, built upon fallacies,
> Produce disillusionment, envy, and strife.
> Open your heart to receive
> God's gift of eternal life,
> A life that overcomes all obstacles
> And is strengthened by God's grace.
> During tough times and in hard places,
> It stands against evil's hellish chase!
> Ah, God has spoken the gospel message;
> Throughout the earth it is proclaimed:
> "I love you! Come to Me. Enter the golden gates!"

September 9

Sorrowful Repentance

"Produce fruit in keeping with repentance." (Luke 3:8a)

Dear Father, help us to produce the fruit of righteousness. Your indwelling love ripens the fruit within our souls to be given away to others in the bond of unity and love. With repentant and thankful hearts, may we continually serve one another in a spirit of cheerful and zealous love, bearing the steadfastness and tenderness of our faithful Lord. Amen.

MEDITATION:
Sorrowful repentance gives way to praise.

> Jesus' love casts a distinctive glow…
> His beauty emits from one's soul.

߷

September 10

Passing the Test

"See, I have refined you, though not as silver; I have tested you in the furnace of affliction." (Isa. 48:10)

Father, You know our hearts require Your wondrous light to expose the deadened corners of our hearts. Father, cast Your redemptive light on our souls. Deliver us from strongholds. Let us rejoice and live in the goodness of Your eternal flame of holy love! Amen.

MEDITATION:
Passing the test requires total trust in and dependence on Christ Jesus our Lord.

> The fury inside quickly unfolded
> And pummeled him low to the ground…
> In great surprise he staggered forward;
> The reason was unfound.
> A darkened cloud swept over him;
> A smile became a frown,
> The former tranquil moments
> Turned upside down.
> The battle he was engaged in
> Was the battle of the mind.
> Character was being tested…
> It was all on the line.
> With God's armor in place,

And God's Word memorized,
The enemy had to flee.
Praise to God was too high a price.

September 11
Holiness and Righteousness

"[T]o rescue us from the hand of our enemies, and to enable us to serve him without fear." (Luke 1:74)

Lord, today, strengthen our hearts so that we may boldly serve You. Renew our minds with the power of Your Word. Deliver us from fear's torment. Increase our faith and deliver us from the trappings of our enemies. Open our minds to receive Your great love driving out fear. Amen.

MEDITATION:
Fear and faith are like oil and water. They don't mix well.

The sweet peace of God is like a refreshing wind on a hot humid day or like a rainbow in the skies to promise us safekeeping when the floodwaters threaten to wash over our anxious souls. Trust gives wings to peace, and in faith we can soar the spiritual heights with Almighty God.

September 12
With the Eyes of Faith

"He has showed, O man, what is good. And what does the Lord require of you? To act justly and to love mercy and to walk humbly with your God." (Mic. 6:8)

Father, will we do what You require of us? May our consciences be cleansed from iniquities and impurities and our hearts purified by Your holy flame as we begin anew. Feeding daily on

Your Word, digesting Truth, transforms our minds. Grant us sensitive spirits that are willing to obey Your tender, spoken Word. May we lift the praises of Jesus higher than the praises of men. Amen.

MEDITATION:
With eyes of faith we can see and know the goodness of God.

> Instruction enters a righteous man's heart:
> Do as I do…in simple lesson form…
> Love is learned by doing what has been shown.

ᴥᔕ ʕᴥ

September 13

God Hears

"'In my distress I called to the Lord, and he answered me. From the depths of the grave I called for help, and you listened to my cry.'"
(Jon. 2:2)

Lord, let our remembrance of Your constant faithfulness bring hope to our souls as we call to You. You hear and answer our cries. With renewed hearts that have been sprinkled by the rains of affliction and brightened by the Sun's Righteousness, to the One Who hears us, we give You honor and reverence as we wait upon You, Lord, and serve You in love. Amen.

MEDITATION:
God hears our cries and feels our pain.

> Our God hears our cries…
> When we are distressed,
> Our God is in the midst,
> Working out good for us.
> In simple childlike faith…
> Trust in God's grace.

ᴥᔕ ʕᴥ

September 14
Deep Roots

"But you have an anointing from the Holy One, and all of you know the truth." (1 John 2:20)

Father, Christ in us *is* the anointing! We are free in Christ...He who is Truth sets us free from the chains of sin and the strongholds that paralyze us. The anointing destroys the yoke. Praise be to God for the gift of His Spirit. Holy One, teach us all things that we might walk in truth. Amen.

MEDITATION:
A lie believed grows deep roots.

> Oftentimes a lie believed entangles emotions,
> sabotaging a life lived fully and expectantly.

September 15
Communion

"[H]e predestined us to be adopted as his sons through Jesus Christ, in accordance with his pleasure and will." (Eph. 1:5)

Father, to think that we could bring You delight and pleasure is a great encouragement to serve You with abandonment. Your love motivates and inspires us. Let Your presence melt my heart, as I meditate on Your goodness and love. Amen.

MEDITATION:
Our Father delights in communion with him.

> To turn away from God is to shut out
> the Holy Light of God's omnipresence.
> Remain open and faithful.
> He takes pleasure in shining light in lives.

September 16

Love Touched Earth

"But you, O Sovereign Lord, deal well with me for your name's sake; out of the goodness of your love, deliver me." (Ps. 109:21)

Father, love is Your moving force...love is Your redemptive power...love spares us from the enemy's venomous gnashing. His bite is not fatal when Your power is great within us. We are made whole by Your great love, as You touch our wounds and heal our souls.

MEDITATION:
Love touched earth with eternal treasure.

> Love thinks about us constantly
> And communes with our spirit.
> Love never fails...
> God's Love is eternal.

September 17

The Lord is Our Keeper

"The Lord watches over you—the Lord is your shade at your right hand." (Ps. 121:5)

O Lord, You encircle me with love. You bear me up in Your powerful arms. I am enthralled with Your beauty. Keeper of my soul, never do You slumber; faithfully You shield me in Your loving care. Amen.

MEDITATION:
The Lord is our Keeper.

> The Lord takes responsibility for my soul.
> He leads me according to His loving-kindness.
> As I yield to the gentleness of God's Spirit,
> The Way is opened unto me for all eternity.

September 18

God's Signature

"The highest heavens belong to the Lord, but the earth he has given to man." (Ps. 115:16)

Dear Father, the earth's resources are precious—a signature of divine love entrusted to us. May we take responsibility in caring for one another, giving You honor and delight and immense pleasure, as we share the love of Christ. Earth resound with the good news of God's love. Rejoice in the Creator! Amen.

MEDITATION:
God's signature bears the scars of Calvary and the triumph of the Resurrection.

> Manifold gifts from God's open hand are discovered in the simplicity and beauty all around us. Let us receive from His hand of mercy all the blessings our Lord has stored up for His children. Our Father's desire is to give His children good and perfect gifts. Let it be our desire to love and bear witness to the Giver.

ಆ ಶ

September 19

Gardener

"You care for the land and water it; you enrich it abundantly. The streams of God are filled with water to provide the people with grain, for so you have ordained it." (Ps. 65:9)

Father, You are everywhere! Your glorious Presence is all around! We rejoice and revel in Your majesty. Lord, in the wonder of Your awesome mercy and grace, we, Your children, rejoice! By Your Spirit, we are empowered to love others, generously sharing the abundance of blessings given. You supply seed to sow. Because

You, O Lord, are in control, we can relax in Your care. Amen.

MEDITATION:
Our Gardener tills our hearts, enriching our lives.

> The earth exists on the abundance of God's mercy.
> Mere human strength is to be pitied, void of God's power and might.

☙ ❧

September 20
Our Merciful Physician

"I said, 'O Lord, have mercy on me; heal me, for I have sinned against you.'" (Ps. 41:4)

Merciful Lord, quicken my soul immediately when I sin. For my soul is in turmoil whenever sin comes into my life. My body is Your temple, and sin desecrates Your holy dwelling place. Allow no ill root to wrap itself around my soul. Expose the hidden things in my life that sadden You. Free me of any self-deception that I may boldly walk in the Spirit. Make my soul healthy, as I continually feed on Your truths and daily put into practice Your principles for abundant living. Amen.

MEDITATION:
Our merciful Physician restores and reinstates.

> Merciful Physician,
> Heal sin's painful pelts
> Lashing our hearts.
> In mercy, remember us.
> In mercy, forgive us.

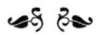

☙ ❧

September 21

In Truth and in Love

"Endure hardship with us like a good soldier of Christ Jesus."
(2 Tim. 2:3)

Dear Jesus, in this world we will suffer. But we do not suffer in vain. You know about our sufferings, and You work mightily in the midst of them. You are good, and we trust in You to work together all things for Your good. It's by Your strength and grace, giving our faith substance and endurance, that we are given the final victory! You will deliver us from all evil and establish our steps on higher ground. For the spiritual plane is supernatural; and the evil of the day is no match against Your prevailing mighty Spirit. Amen.

MEDITATION:
Our Father confronts us in truth and in love.

> God's voice melts the frozen river of despair
> and brings rhythmic beauty to the flowing river
> of peace.

September 22

The Right of Way

"'Woe to the world because of the things that cause people to sin! Such things must come, but woe to the man through whom they come!'" (Matt. 18:7)

Father, temptations will come, but chastisement will follow the evil deeds of man. Dear Lord, show us the way out that we might escape worldly temptations. Deliver us from our fleshly impulses, and bring us into a deeper spiritual awareness of practicing and developing greater intimacy with You. Amen.

MEDITATION:
Yield to Christ; Christ always has the "right of way."
The greatest treasure discovered on the journey of

faith is manifested in the traces of God's love experienced in simple, everyday happenings. For the whole earth is interwoven in the divine tapestry of His redeeming love.

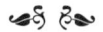

❦ ❧

September 23
God's Redemption

"I will search for the lost and bring back the strays. I will bind up the injured and strengthen the weak, but the sleek and the strong I will destroy. I will shepherd the flock with justice." (Ezek. 34:16)

Father, we praise You in meditative silences and in joyous shouts of song! Blessed is Your holy Name…now and forevermore. My heart is still before You, reassured and comforted, as I gaze into the loveliness of Your face and wait on Your sweet, gentle voice to whisper to my spirit: "Be still and know that I am God" (Ps. 46:10a). Amen.

MEDITATION:
God's redemption brings eternal blessings.

>Enticed by temporal things,
>Void of God's richest blessings,
>Anxiety rose within my soul!
>I cried, "Lord, I lost my way…
>I need Your help today."
>His forgiving face appeared,
>As a Morning Star,
>Carrying me gently
>Homeward bound
>On angels' wings.

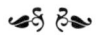

❦ ❧

September 24

Abba, Father

"Those who know your name will trust in you, for you, Lord, have never forsaken those who seek you." (Ps. 9:10)

Lord, the tenderness of Your love is initiated, and we are brought into a growing relationship of eternal love. As we begin to really know You and learn how to listen for Your soft voice, those inner stirrings, trust is being developed. When You command the storms to be still or deliver us from peril, we see Your hand moving and we move closer to You. When all hope seems to vanish, we discover our hope is in You; and it's in the waiting room of faith that trust gives birth. Lord, we grow in grace and trust in Your name even during the seasons of dormancy. Amen.

MEDITATION:
Abba, Father, is a name of trust and intimacy.

When my thoughts become entangled,
God's Word breaks apart a link of error
That would gain strength if left unchecked.
Clarity is given and I am free!

Father, trust and intimacy are gained—
Sustained with love that is pure and true.
Discipline is needed and truth is meted—
Covered with unquenchable love from You.

❦

September 25

Sustenance from God

"Then Jesus said to the centurion, 'Go! It will be done just as you believed it would.' And his servant was healed at that very hour." (Matt. 8:13)

Father, grant me the faith of the centurion. The timing and execution of Your perfect will is in Your hands. Teach me to "mount up" with wings of faith that I might dispel fear and live in Your perfect peace. I submit to Your authority and seek Your face. Oh, help me, God. Amen.

MEDITATION:
Sustenance from man is temporal and fades with time, but sustenance from God is everlasting.

> When God opens wide His hand
> And invites us to take what we need,
> What will come first?
> Faith or greed?

September 26

Complacency Destroys

"[Moses] said to them, 'Take to heart all the words I have solemnly declared to you this day, so that you may command your children to obey carefully all the words of this law.'" (Deut. 32:46)

O God, You instruct us to think on Your precepts, that we might diligently teach them to our children. Lord, please give me an instructive tongue. May my spiritual legacy be built upon love, expressed tenderly yet uncompromisingly and continuously to future generations. Help me to clearly state the truth, not withholding any given word of warning or reproof. Amen.

MEDITATION:
Complacency destroys God's momentous working in our lives. Keeping our hearts and minds obedient to Christ Jesus opens His channels of love to many.

> Lord, help us to never be self-satisfied,
> Giving way to falsehood and foolish pride.
> Prompt us to stir our spiritual gifts inside…
> And resonate with love,
> That You might be glorified!

September 27

The Creativeness of God

"In the beginning God created the heavens and the earth." (Gen. 1:1)

Almighty God! Who can describe Your ways? And Your goodness has no end. O God, in the splendor of Your breathtaking design, the earth and the heavens were formed. One breath from You and the universe was created. Amidst the beauty and majesty of Your world, You have fashioned man to glorify Your name. Praise rings forth throughout "the heavens and the earth" to the Author of life, now and forevermore. Amen.

MEDITATION:
The creativeness of God is experienced by sight, touch, smell, taste, and hearing.

> Over the face of the earth
> Creation is on display.
> His powers at work
> Need not be overlooked
> Because of our worries today.
> Let's focus our thoughts on the beginning
> When God spoke and it was finished...
> O God's powerful word is truth;
> His power will never diminish.

September 28

Wise in Our Own Eyes

"For who knows what is good for a man in life, during the few and meaningless days he passes through like a shadow? Who can tell him what will happen under the sun after he is gone?" (Eccl. 6:12)

Lord, we desperately need Your unlimited wisdom! We rely on Your perfect knowledge and understanding working through us, dear Lord. We seek Your counsel and meditate on Scripture. We inquire about Your will for our lives and then make decisions that are Christ-honoring. Bring all our desires in perfect harmony with Your desires, Lord, for wisdom remains connected with You, wonderful Counselor. Amen.

MEDITATION:
When we are wise in our own eyes, our eyes become blinded by arrogance.

> Make me a blessing, faithful and true,
> An object of mercy flowing from You.
> Make me a blessing, fill me with love;
> Pour out Your Spirit from the heavens above.
>
> Make me a blessing; to You I belong,
> Placed in Your family, steadfast and strong!
> Make me a blessing, wise in Your ways,
> Seeking Your will, not my way.

September 29

Heavenward

"'He made the earth by his power; he founded the world by his wisdom and stretched out the heavens by his understanding.'" (Jer. 51:15)

Father, the universe was created by Your great power, wisdom, and understanding. You establish our ways and make steady our steps, giving light to our paths. Why do we fear the reproach of man and doubt the deliverance wrought by Your right arm? Lord, help us to relax in the ever-present knowledge of Your love, daily seeking Your wisdom and trusting in Your understanding ways. Amen.

MEDITATION:
Looking heavenward.

> Looking heavenward, acknowledging God's
> great handiwork of moon and stars, we are

awestruck with the magnificence of His creation. Like credits following a great performance or a masterful achievement or a great accomplishment, the heavens glow like a neon sign flashing: "No greater work on earth or in the heavens will surpass the inexpressible account of creation by God's great power."

September 30

Wings of Love

"For it is written: 'He will command his angels concerning you to guard you carefully.'" (Luke 4:10)

Your Word, O Lord, is a powerful sword. We can brandish our weapon against evil schemes and deceptive strategies. Fear must flee when faith stands unwavering. Your ministering spirits are dispatched to watch over our comings and goings, to obey Your instructions and commands. O Lord, You are our refuge, and we are kept safe by Your powerful right arm. Jesus, our High Priest, intercedes for us. Amen.

MEDITATION:
Mercy is sent on wings of love.

God releases the cloudburst…
Showers of blessings fall.
The balm of Gilead heals…
At the sound of His call.

October 1

True Character

"Who can discern his errors? Forgive my hidden faults." (Ps. 19:12)

Father, eyes peering into my heart, You reveal my true inner-self, and then with loving-kindness You change the old to new.

You meet me with overwhelming love and acceptance, and all my defenses come tumbling down. Your love flowing through me satisfies my soul and heals my wounds. O Lamb of God, Your light dispels the darkness. Amen.

MEDITATION:
Testing reveals our true character.

> I believed I was the person
> Whose reflection in the mirror
> Appeared stable and whole,
> Until God's image came into view.
> Then I beheld, in my heart's mirror,
> The Truthful One facing me—
> Now my own reflection was askew.
> Holding on to Truth, I cleaved to One
> Who said, *"Take My yoke;*
> *I will walk with you."*

❧ ☙

October 2

Relinquishment of Self

"He is like a tree planted by streams of water, which yields its fruit in season and whose leaf does not wither. Whatever he does prospers." (Ps. 1:3)

Lord, happiness is found in trusting You. Allowing Your Word to wash over our daily cares and anxieties frees us to be open to Your voice and calling. Your song of faithfulness constantly replenishes our souls with hope. And as we grow, moment by moment, in the wondrous spiritual life, we find happiness in being vitally connected to You. Amen.

MEDITATION:
Wholeness begins with the relinquishment of self to God.

Life flowing from Christ maintains the wholeness of the Body. When we choose to block His flow, like a twisted garden hose, we suffer from spiritual blockage.

October 3

Living Water

"From the fruit of his lips a man is filled with good things as surely as the work of his hands rewards him." (Prov. 12:14)

Father, whatever we speak will prove to be a blessing or a curse. Today may I speak words of encouragement, words of victory, words of hope, and words of faith. Your are faithful Father, giving us abundant life and eternal hope. I give to You all that I am. Multiply the seed and increase Your harvest of goodness and mercy, that many may come to know Your Son. Amen.

MEDITATION:
Dry, barren ground springs alive with Living Water.

Apart from Christ's abiding love,
We would be driven by selfishness.
Living Water satisfies our deepest needs,
And our hands reach out to others.

October 4

Remaining Close to God

"Let the morning bring me word of your unfailing love, for I have put my trust in you. Show me the way I should go, for to you I lift up my soul." (Ps. 143:8)

I love You, my Lord and my Strength! Lord, place Your desires in my heart. May my walking path be clear, O Lord, and my steps steady and sure. Give me courage to go where You lead and the endurance to remain faithful where You place me. Amen.

MEDITATION:

Remaining close to God softens my heart to hear His gentle voice.
>Keep me on track, Lord,
>Away from clamoring forces
>Competing against the light.
>Still my soul with joy, Lord,
>And fill my cup with gladness,
>As You speak to me in the night.

October 5

He Who Searches Hearts

"'And you, my son Solomon, acknowledge the God of your father, and serve him with wholehearted devotion and with a willing mind, for the Lord searches every heart and understands every motive behind the thoughts. If you seek him, he will be found by you; but if you forsake him, he will reject you forever.'" (1 Chron. 28:9)

Lord Jesus, our faithful and devoted Shepherd, Who is the promise of wholeness and the fulfillment of the Scriptures, receive our praises in prayers of thanksgiving, in joyful singing, and in quiet meditations of the heart. Our hope is in the blessed name of Jesus, and, with hearts purified by His love, we are free to rejoice! Amen.

MEDITATION:

Our Guardian knows the depth of our heart's despair and deceitfulness. He Who searches hearts also finds and restores the lost intimacy of broken fellowship with Him.

>God's eternal love searches the depth of our intense pain and despair and uplifts our burdens onto His shoulders. We are free to trust His ways and walk close by His side, unencumbered and untangled, because of God's deliverance through Jesus Christ.

October 6

God's Wisdom

"'I have installed my King on Zion, my holy hill.'" (Ps. 2:6)

Jesus Christ…immovable…unchangeable…eternal. O God, You have placed leaders on earth to do great works in Your name, as the Spirit work's mightily through them. No amount of opposition can change Your plans. Today may we submit to Your authority and uphold our leaders in prayer, bringing everything to the throne of Almighty God. Give us the faith to answer Your call, the courage to fulfill the tasks given us, and the grace to endure. Amen.

MEDITATION:
God's wisdom sets in motion what's necessary to fulfill His purposes.

> When we don't understand His ways
> And confusion floods our minds,
> Still trust…
> When attempted explanations offered
> Fail to erase painful blank stares,
> Still trust…
> When victory cries its winning shout,
> Uplifted hands will celebrate,
> "In God we trust!"

October 7

At the Crossroads

"Remember to extol his work, which men have praised in song." (Job 36:24)

O Lord, may Your grace working in us display Your splendor and mercy. When we are slandered or wronged, grant us forgiving hearts, because we trust in You and bear Your glorious name. May the sneers of unbelieving men be changed to reverent fear and trembling wonder, as You pierce hearts with the love of Christ.

Amen.

MEDITATION:
At the crossroads of indecision, stop, seek, and go.

> People are watching...
> What we say,
> Where we go,
> And what we do
> Count for Christ.

October 8

The Splendor of God

"For to us a child is born, to us a son is given, and the government will be on his shoulders. And he will be called Wonderful Counselor, Mighty God, Everlasting Father, Prince of Peace." (Isa. 9:6)

You are everything to me, Lord. There is no one like You. Who can describe Your beauty? Who can fully take in the magnitude of Your love that surrounds us? Lord, Your presence gives us peace—Your nearness comforts us. Your light shines forth on earth, warming cold hearts with the covering of Your Spirit. Amen.

MEDITATION:
The splendor of God is manifested in the lives of His children.

> God's vast richness is woven
> Into the fabric of our souls—
> A pattern of His handiwork
> For you and for me...
> Set apart for God's purposes
> And anointed are we,
> Attentive to instructions
> From Christ our glorious King!

October 9

Joy is God's Gift

"The prospect of the righteous is joy, but the hopes of the wicked come to nothing." (Prov. 10:28)

Lord, there is hopeful expectation for those who abide in a personal relationship with You. To fulfill our purpose in life, to be content and satisfied with what we are doing, using our talents and gifts, is to achieve the highest goal of all—walking in step with You. I would rather have joy, knowing that our relationship is prosperous, than the disappointment and emptiness in my soul from traveling a divergent path. I love You, Lord, and I am comforted to know that there is joy in the journey. Amen.

MEDITATION:
Joy is God's gift to us. It lifts and releases our expressions of delight.

> Circumstances cannot touch the immovable and invincible Spirit in us. He is stability in an unstable world—a place of certainty and solace. Jealous and protective is our Father. Joy is the outward expression of rhapsody, orchestrated by God, in our hearts.

October 10

The Fragrance of Christ

"A kindhearted woman gains respect, but ruthless men gain only wealth." (Prov. 11:16)

Lord, it's not in what we say, but in what we say and do. Teach us to grow beyond ourselves, embracing someone's pain or grief or fear, reaching others with Your outstretched arms of sincere love. Move us to compassion and mercy and energize our spirits with Your strength. Amen.

MEDITATION:
The fragrance of Christ is like a rose touched by heavenly dew.

> Beauty unfolds one petal at a time
> As inward growth takes form.
> Our basic need,
> In Christ received
> Our blossoming fully adorned.

October 11

The Fuel that Ignites the Wick

"You, O Lord, keep my lamp burning; my God turns my darkness into light." (Ps. 18:28)

Lord Jesus Christ, Your Holy Spirit gives light to our bodies. Your glory shines upon our frames of dust, illuminating our bodies like shining stars. As we yield to Your light, darkness flees and we are free…a testimony of Your power and grace working in us. Time spent with You redirects our thoughts and realigns our steps to follow Your steps. Peace radiates our lives when You shine on us, Lord. Make us light bearers, zealous to boldly hold high our torches, ignited by Your Spirit, bringing light to the dark corners around us. In Jesus' name, we pray. Amen.

MEDITATION:
God's love is the fuel that ignites the wick.

> One look, just a glance, one life-giving breath,
> our life is altered forever. Life bursts forth with
> indomitable hope and great expectation, like
> the timely changing seasons, full of promise and
> adventure, awakening in us a new beginning.
> Reach for Him. It's time to celebrate the reality
> of His love.

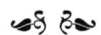

October 12
Life is Meant to be Lived with Christ

"[A]nd live a life of love, just as Christ loved us and gave himself up for us as a fragrant offering and sacrifice to God." (Eph. 5:2)

Lord, You have commanded us to love one another as You love us. Teach us to serve in love, even while undergoing pain and hardship, misunderstanding, and loss. Grant us the grace to identify with Your sorrow, responding in loving compassion. Help us, O God. Amen.

MEDITATION:
Life is meant to be lived with Christ. Living "a life of love" is the backdrop to every scene, choosing good over evil.

> Painted scenes on the horizons of my mind…
> Memories colored with brushstrokes of yesteryear,
> Where laughter wells up from deep inside,
> As thoughts reveal humorous lines…
> Or tears of discomfort slip down a cheek,
> When the heart still aches, the soul still weeps…
> Our fondest times are those well spent
> With loving friends whose hearts have met
> Our lonely burdens or sought after advice…
> And believed life is meant to be lived with Christ!

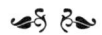

⋄⋄⋄

October 13
Right to the Finish Line!

"This is what the Lord says: 'Maintain justice and do what is right, for my salvation is close at hand and my righteousness will soon be revealed.'" (Isa. 56:1)

Father, a command spoken in love and simplicity, yet, apart from

Your love, impossible to do. We desperately need our minds renewed daily. Let our thoughts and actions reflect Your Spirit in us. Etch into our consciences the true meaning of obedience. And when we are tempted to take the easy way out, bring to our remembrances the Cross. Amen.

MEDITATION:
God's commands go the distance...right to the finish line!

> His call is to *"keep going."*
> His cry is, *"Never quit!"*
> With encouragement
> Our Lord says,
> *"What I've begun,*
> *I will complete!"*

ಸ್ ಬಿ

October 14

With God's Anointing

"Today I have made you a fortified city, an iron pillar and a bronze wall to stand against the whole land." (Jer. 1:18a)

Thank You, dear Lord, for Your wondrous life-giving Word that energizes and uplifts us out of the doldrums. Your Spirit brings wellness to our bodies and wholeness to our minds. I praise You, Lord, for reaching out to us and embracing our fears and anxieties with Your love. We are touched by Your grace and strengthened by Your Spirit. Amen.

MEDITATION:
With God's anointing, no task is impossible to perform.

> When the choice is made to obey Him,
> God's Spirit powerfully works within
> To complete the tasks at hand,
> For His purpose and design.

ಸ್ ಬಿ

October 15
Our Lives Tell a Story

"Here am I, and the children the Lord has given me. We are signs and symbols in Israel from the Lord Almighty, who dwells in Mount Zion." (Isa. 8:18)

Lord, what an awesome privilege to be chosen as "signs and symbols" in a depraved world. Help us to eagerly serve You with integrity and godly joy in all our circumstances. Quicken our spirits to the slightest disconnecting from our union with You, O God, allowing us to feel the agony of being disjointed from You. Because of Your great love and compassion, may this needful discomfort create in us a response to cleave tightly to You, lest we spoil the testimony of Your "signs and symbols." Amen.

MEDITATION:
Our lives tell a story about Christ or about self.

> Be still my soul; God is working, exploring the
> depth of my sinful heart.
> Deep down inside His revealing light marks
> the area to be incised.
> (A little cutting away, and some gentle shaping, too.) The wisdom of
> God's transforming touch is changing me into
> a trophy for my King!

જી ઉ

October 16
A Wavering Faith

"If you do not stand firm in your faith, you will not stand at all." (Isa. 7:9b)

Jesus, to take a stand in our faith means full surrender. Any hesitation will cause a negative response and outcome. Lord, please strengthen our bodies and renew our minds as we daily meet with

You in prayer and meditation. Then we will be ready to face the storms of life with the "blessed assurance" of Your peace. Grant us godly confidence as we hold on to faith. Amen.

MEDITATION:
A wavering faith is like sinking sand.

> Standing for Christ sometimes means feeling the discomfort of walking away from crude joking, gossiping, or questionable practices. Oftentimes our choices will be in conflict with the majority, and chiding and angry mockery will be expressed. But during these momentary afflictions, as the barbs pierce our hearts, we must remember the One who was pierced so that we might have the "fullness" of Christ (Col. 2:9–10).

October 17

Overcomers

"The Lord is with me; he is my helper. I will look in triumph on my enemies." (Ps. 118:7)

Lord, I am so thankful for Your presence. You bring restoration to my soul. In You, Lord, I find solace and comfort. Inner calmness comes as thoughts of You flood my mind. All my enemies on every level—physically, emotionally, mentally, and spiritually—are defeated by Your name. Help me walk in truth and in the authority of Your Son. In Jesus' name. Amen.

MEDITATION:
Overcomers come under the authority of Christ.

> To surrender seems like giving up:
> Letting go…coming undone…quitting.
> But there's much to achieve God's way,
> For Christ sees surrender

Through the Father's eyes,
In trust and in believing faith.

October 18

The Embrace of a Lifetime

"My soul clings to you; your right hand upholds me." (Ps. 63:8)

Precious Lord, I press in to be nearer to You and I am satisfied by Your loving embrace. Peace permeates my soul, the quiet and affirming knowledge of Your hand upon me. Daily I must come to You and "in all [my] ways acknowledge [You]" (Prov. 3:6). For You are the anchor of my soul, and in Your presence I am safely kept. Amen.

MEDITATION:
The embrace of a lifetime begins and finishes with Almighty God.

Wrap Your love around my soul,
And preserve it for eternity!
For Your presence is my portion,
Boundless love to infinity!

October 19

Truth Savored

"An honest answer is like a kiss on the lips." (Prov. 24:26)

Speaking the truth brings sweetness to our souls. Lord, help us to speak sincere words. Give us ears and hearts that are open to listening and understanding. As we store up the riches of Your Word, may we always be ready to share Your insights with those who ask for our counsel. Almighty Counselor, it's Your wisdom, guidance, and counsel that we seek. Amen.

MEDITATION:
Truth savored is a lasting remembrance.

The aroma of fresh dripped coffee permeates the air, beckoning the senses to indulge in its flavor. Cookies baking or other favorite foods tantalize the taste buds into action. Truth is very similar. We consider what we are hearing, recall past experiences, and discern the truth.

October 20

Selfless Prayers

"Christ is the end of the law so that there may be righteousness for everyone who believes." (Rom. 10:4)

Father, thank You for Your redeeming grace. Grace that saves! O what a wondrous gift is salvation! Righteousness comes from Christ and not of our own. May we be fervent in prayer and zealous for the cause of Christ. Amen.

MEDITATION:
Selfless prayers reflect God's grace.

Tears of incense rise to God's throne...
Jesus intercedes; He hears our moans.
Selfless prayers reflect God's grace,
Desiring Christ to be first place.

October 21

We Become What God Ordains and Purposes

"I have become its servant by the commission God gave me to present to you the word of God in its fullness." (Col. 1:25)

Dear Father, You have given Your children the great commission: "Therefore go and make disciples of all nations" (Matt.28:19a). May we be found faithful in all that we do: faithful in speech and in deeds, and in our relationship with You. Let us reflect Your love and goodness that others might yearn to know You. Remind us, O Lord, that we are walking testimonies. Amen.

MEDITATION:

As we trust God with our lives, we become what God ordains and purposes.

> Fit the pieces of our lives together;
> Lord, bring wholeness to our souls.
> Come and breathe upon our frames;
> Let the lamp of Christ brightly glow.
> New life is given to each one
> Who bows their knee to You.
> *The Great Commission* is given,
> To spread the Good News:
> *"Know I am with you always,*
> *My Spirit is in you."*

⊰ ⊱

October 22

His Lordship

"Your hands made me and formed me; give me understanding to learn your commands." (Ps. 119:73)

Father, You uniquely designed each person. We are made by Your great wisdom, fashioned by Your wondrous hands of true love. You were there in the very beginning of our conception, with a unique plan and purpose for each one of us. May our life events be ordered and guided by You. Keep us from wallowing in the deceitfulness of our hearts and its regrets. Teach us to completely trust You with our lives, yielded to Your authority, heavenly Father. Amen.

MEDITATION:

We owe our lives, our total surrender, to His Lordship. He is faithful to bring to pass all that He purposes in our lives.

> God, a master of detail, whose passion towards

mankind cost Him His signature in blood,
sealed every promise with yes!
Go forward with trust and expectant hope!

October 23

When We are in Error

"A rebuke impresses a man of discernment more than a hundred lashes a fool." (Prov. 17:10)

Lord, when our hearts are aligned to do Your will, they become sensitive and tender to Your ways. Any slight shifting from our firm stand in Christ, pierces our consciences. Therefore, a word spoken in truth and in love captures our attentions. Although a rebuke is unsettling, filled with godly insight, it gives way to inner change and growth. Father, thank You for sending people who "speak…the truth in love" (Eph. 4:15). Amen.

MEDITATION:
When we are in error, our merciful God sends warnings.

> Break away and come with Me…
> Time together is needed desperately.
> Listen to the words I speak to you…
> Repentance comes from abiding truth.

October 24

Begin with Daily Thoughts of God's Goodness

"But be sure to fear the Lord and serve him faithfully with all your heart; consider what great things he has done for you. Yet if you persist in doing evil, both you and your king will be swept away." (1 Sam. 12:24–25)

Eternal God! Lord of Salvation! Holy God who dwelt among men as a man, You are as near to us as our breath. Who can understand the magnitude of Your greatness? O Blessed Trinity, how can we express our thankfulness for Your marvelous grace? How can we know the meaning of suffering without entering into Your suffering? For You teach us to be burden bearers and compassionate servants. Even in our darkest hour, You are always with us, comforting our souls. Teach us to rejoice in the tough places, giving us the strength to persevere along our journey of faith. Amen.

MEDITATION:
Begin with daily thoughts of God's goodness and finish with a lifetime of rejoicing. For He is our Father and in Him is great mercy and grace!

> O Father, receive our praise and thanksgiving!
> For Your whisperings of joyous love touch
> Our hearts, uplifting our souls with cleansing tears
> Of gladness, as we consider Your marvelous ways!

October 25

To Be Identified with Christ

"I have been reminded of your sincere faith, which first lived in your grandmother Lois and in your mother Eunice and, I am persuaded, now lives in you also." (2 Tim. 1:5)

Father, lead me through both the rough terrain and the meadows with thanksgiving on my lips, as I recall Your redeeming love and faithfulness. Make me a faithful witness to Your empowerment, and an obedient servant in Your kingdom. Bring me into appointed places—places marked by Your wisdom. Step by step, Lord, lead me on! And when my earthly journey is over, I'll see the panoramic view of Your glorious plan for my life, knowing that purpose fulfilled is its own sweet reward! Amen.

MEDITATION:
To be identified with Christ is great honor!

Step by step God leads us...
By His wisdom we succeed.
Casting doubt to earthly measure,
Values are kept along the way.
And we give honor to God,
Who is guiding our temporal stay.

October 26

Golden Love-Ties

"Let us not give up meeting together, as some are in the habit of doing, but let us encourage one another—and all the more as you see the Day approaching." (Heb. 10:25)

Lord Jesus, help us to persevere, remaining faithful in fellowship. With Your strength we can make it and can help spur one another on. As Your love is released through us, we become aware of the power in selfless giving—encouraging one another, praying for one another, and tearing down strongholds that create barriers to fulfilling our God-given potential. May we be found faithful, Jesus, for Your name's sake. Amen.

MEDITATION:
Golden love-ties wrap around our bundles of burdens, as we gather together in His sweet fellowship.

Do you carry a heavy burden?
It's a load not to carry alone.
God's field has laborers of love
Willing to share it with you...
If only they knew.

October 27

Words of Affirmation

"'Don't be afraid,'" the prophet answered. "'Those who are with us are more than those who are with them.'" (2 Kings 6:16)

Father, open our eyes to Your sovereign protection. We are precious in Your sight. Keep us mindful of Your faithful promises and Your covenant of love. Help us to accept and make application to Your Word, digesting the truths, confidently entrusting our lives to Your care. Father, remind us that we are held responsible and accountable for how we spent our time on earth using the gifts given us. Grant us the courage to carry out the tasks set before us. Amen.

MEDITATION:
Words of affirmation burn God's truths into our minds.

> God's Word declares the truth to open minds prepared to receive knowledge and understanding. We eagerly search to find significance and meaning for our lives. And we are not disappointed as we discover a land mine of wealth found in the wisdom of God, prompting an exploration of reevaluation and reexamination of our values, in which we encounter God's purposes and plans for our lives.

October 28

His Presence

"Do you not realize that Christ Jesus is in you—unless, of course, you fail the test?" (2 Cor. 13:5b)

Lord Jesus, with You working in us, by faith, we can move mountains. You take the hard things and make them simple, exposing the fears that beset us, disarming them and making us "more than conquerors" (Rom. 8:37). We are the righteousness of God, because You, Merciful Lord, have taken our sin and, in Your body, nailed it to the Cross. All things become possible when You live in us. Just say the word, and what we find impossible in human terms, will be accomplished through Your Spirit. Only open our hearts to applying Your truth, and amazing things will begin to happen. Amen.

MEDITATION:
God's amazing love quiets our fears with the calming effect of His presence.

> Nearer to my heart, Glorious Savior, You
> desire to be—
> Involved in daily decisions—walking closer,
> closer with me.
> Knowing what lies ahead, O Creator Who
> created me,
> You reach out to guide my life with grace and
> mercy—
> Abundantly channeling love richly flowing.

❧ ☙

October 29

Invite Joy into Your Heart

"A cheerful look brings joy to the heart, and good news gives health to the bones." (Prov. 15:30)

Lord, teach us to surrender our burdens to Your care, so that we do not become vessels of despair. Fill our hearts with gladness, and shine brightly in our lives that we might be faithful encouragers to those experiencing tumult and pain. One look of love can embrace a lonely or discouraged soul, adding a few moments of joy. Keep us diligent in prayer as we await Your return. Amen.

MEDITATION:
Focusing on Jesus can change dreary into cheery. Inviting Joy into your heart produces a continual feast of thanksgiving.

> Blank stares can convey joyless messages.
> Oftentimes an impatient look or a shrug expresses indifference. Avoidance sends loud
> signals. Somber tears signal distress. But what

can warm the heart? Ah! A smile…sincere and spontaneously expressed. Now add a gentle squeeze of the hand and you've exchanged despair with hopefulness.

October 30
No Greater Compensation

"Instead of their shame my people will receive a double portion, and instead of disgrace they will rejoice in their inheritance." (Isa. 61:7a)

Father, thank You for healing our wounded souls—our minds, our wills, and our emotions. Only You have the ability to completely restore us to wholeness. You know our condition and Your grace meets our needs. Not only do we receive what we have lost, but You double what has been taken from us. Almighty God, our Provider, we bow to the honor of Your glorious name. The goodness and wholeness that You give make the former shame and pain look dim. Amen.

MEDITATION:
No greater compensation is given than what is received from Christ.

> We praise the name
> Of the One Who came
> To set us free from sin.
> A valiant Warrior,
> A Shield before us,
> Empowering us within.
> Replacing our shame,
> Reviving our dreams,
> Christ's riches are given…
> "On earth as it is in heaven" (Matt. 6:10b).

October 31

The Hard Spots in Life

"Some time later God tested Abraham." (Gen. 22:1a)

Lord, You know the person on the inside longing to stretch and to grow and to follow You. When we are tested, the condition of our heart is revealed. Will You find us faithful? Faith comes alive as we trust You through adversity and pain. Your wisdom will guide our steps. I pray that our obedience will follow Your calling. Amen.

MEDITATION:
The hard spots in life prepare us for the bright spots in the future.

> God, in holiness and loveliness, dispenses
> golden opportunities for change to take place
> in our lives. Many of these changes require
> painful stretching and reshaping. Purification
> requires a Refiner's fire. Hold fast to the
> Refiner who has His hand upon you. Seize
> every opportunity to shine for Him. We are a
> testament of His love and faithfulness.

November 1

His Ways are Glorious

"Find rest, O my soul, in God alone; my hope comes from him." (Ps. 62:5)

O Glorious Lord, we find rest for our tattered and frayed emotions, for our minds and wills, in Your everlasting arms of love. As our souls cling to You, we discover that healing is taking place on the inside. Grant us the strength and courage to allow You to perform a complete healing work in our lives. Our hope rests in the knowledge of Your great love toward us, Father. By Your grace we can be still, allowing You to work mightily through us! Amen.

MEDITATION:
We rest in God as we yield all of our thoughts and cares to Christ.

> It is not a weak thing
> To yield to One so strong!
> Love and honor go before us
> As we bow before His throne.
> Desire motivates our steps…
> With grateful tears we sing:
> "The joy of the Lord is [my] strength" (Neh. 8:10)…
> All praise to Christ, the risen King!

November 2

Quiet Assurance

"It is God who arms me with strength and makes my way perfect." (2 Sam. 22:33)

O God, thank You for Your garment of sustaining strength that uplifts our soul. We lift up the name of Jesus singing praises to our Lord. You clear paths for our feet to trod safely. We are armed with Your Word, edified and sustained by the power of prayer. Surely, we are covered by Your strength. We have victory in You! Amen.

MEDITATION:
Strength is the quiet assurance of the fullness of God inside us.

> Some trust in themselves, but I dare not
> Forsake the wisdom God has wrought.
> Clearly stated in His Word
> Are messages that must be heard:
> *Christ in us*—we must choose,
> O believer, we cannot lose.

November 3

The Composer of My Soul

"The Lord will fulfill his purpose for me; your love, O Lord, endures forever—do not abandon the works of your hands."
(Ps. 138:8)

Lord Jesus, what comfort Your Word brings to my soul just knowing You reign on earth and in my life! Lord, unfold, step by step, Your divine plan, giving me rich insights into Your amazing grace. May the talents You have given me be multiplied in Your kingdom. Lead me according to Your purposes. O Lord, how magnificent and lovely You are—powerfully and wondrously You move. Remaining the same now and forevermore, Your faithfulness is unmatched. Amen.

MEDITATION:
Jesus is the composer of my soul—a song in the night birthing hope for the dawn.

> Jesus' promises are trustworthy—therefore it
> is done. Our part is to trust with expectancy
> and to listen attentively to our Father's gentle
> inner prompting. We will recognize His voice,
> for we are His children. We need not fear. Our
> Father is near. Obediently we step out and trust
> His leading, remembering that wherever we
> step, He takes the step with us. "The Lord will
> fulfill his purpose for me."

෴

November 4

Sacrifice

"Sacrifice thank offerings to God, fulfill your vows to the Most High." (Ps. 50:14)

Father, teach us the meaning of sacrifice as we give away our money, time, and talents. As we fix our eyes on the Cross, let our hearts be broken. Fill us with the precious fragrance of Christ—all that embodies Him—that we might pour out Your goodness from these jars of clay. You deserve our very best. Let our vows of love and commitment rise before You. Amen.

MEDITATION:
To sacrifice is to give your best.

> God sacrificed His only Son
> To pay our debt in blood.
> Gladly give your best away—
> Give God devoted love.

November 5

An Inward Condition

"He who sacrifices thank offerings honors me, and he prepares the way so that I may show him the salvation of God." (Ps. 50:23)

Lord Jesus, we come before You with our sacrifices of praise and thanksgiving. May our hearts be pure, and our consciences free, as we proclaim our love for You. For to love You is to obey You. O Lord, may we take every opportunity to honor You with great love and devotion—with our voices and our deeds. Teach us selfless giving. All we have comes from Your righteous hand. May we open our hands and give. Amen.

MEDITATION:
God perceives the outward expression of an inward condition.

> Truth spills out of the human heart like water
> cascading down a mountain. Everything is in
> full view. God sees and knows us. He sends the
> convicting power of His Spirit to bring change
> in our lives. Change is sometimes painful—
> unwanted habits are hard to eliminate. Change
> is a lifelong process. But to enjoy the fullness
> of God, our hearts must be fully yielded to

Him. Our sacrifices are the measure of our willingness to put God first place in our lives.

November 6

God is Our Weight Bearer

"To the roots of the mountains I sank down; the earth beneath barred me in forever." (Jon. 2:6a)

O God, only You could possibly know the depth of our cries. "A man of sorrows" (Isa. 53:3), You cried out for all humanity. You know our pain. When we plunge low in the valley of despair, You stoop down to grasp our hands, pulling us upward into Your bosom of love. With great compassion we are rescued. Where would we be without Your consuming love penetrating our hearts and minds? Amen.

MEDITATION:
God is our weight bearer when physical or mental distress weighs us down.

God will come underneath our load and lift it higher. He bears all things for us. Just as a weightlifter lifts heavy weights, resting them in their cradle, God bears our weights, allowing rest for our weary souls.

November 7

Turning to God

"So I turned to the Lord God and pleaded with him in prayer and petition, in fasting, and in sackcloth and ashes." (Daniel 9:3)

Lord, teach us to be like Daniel was, turning to You in boldness and confidence, with the urgency of our prayers and petitions, knowing that You hear us and care for us. With thankful hearts we enter Your throne room of grace, casting all cares upon Your mercy. We empty ourselves so that we may receive Your wisdom, guidance, instruction, and comfort. Yielding to You, our hearts fill with peace. Our lives are held in the delicate balance of Your loving hands, and it is there we are kept safe, while encouraged to grow and to be stretched. When we turn to You, Lord God, we turn to truth, life, and hope. You offer us what the world could never give. Amen.

MEDITATION:
Turning to God needs to be a daily, natural occurrence.

> I had no one…
> I turned to You.
> Offended not,
> In love You drew
> Me close to You.
> Now I know
> My Lord is love.
> To Love I turn…
> To God above.

ಊ§ ಏ

November 8

The Real Person

"[H]e who forms the hearts of all, who considers everything they do." (Ps. 33:15)

Father, You touch the very core of our beings, and we are changed. Your watchful eyes behold everything we do, giving attentive thought to every detail of our lives. Why do we sometimes behave as though You are not with us? For we could never hide from Your presence. Your power and strength go before us. We are safe and secure in Your care. May we not resist the visitations of Your Holy Spirit. His new song in our hearts brings us life-giving direction. Open our eyes to see whether we are too busy or basking in idleness. Teach us to choose balance in our lives and not embrace extremes. Amen.

MEDITATION:
God knows the real person inside.

> Lord, uncover what You've made…
> Remove the protective layers.
> Expose the hidden self
> Wrapped in worldly cares.
> Lord, You're the Architect
> Who designed this form for You.
> Reveal Your vision…
> Occupy each and every room.

November 9

Sealed until Redemption

"Bless all his skills, O Lord, and be pleased with the work of his hands." (Deut. 33:11a)

O Lord, pour out Your blessings on Your children. Achieve through us Your good purposes so that whatever our hands touch, Your will and might are working through us. Cast Your light upon us and take pleasure in work done in Your name. Amen.

MEDITATION:
We are protected, preserved, and approved by the Holy Spirit—sealed until redemption.

> Authentic Christianity is evidenced when
> reliance on the Holy Spirit takes top priority in
> our lives. Godly choices are made as we
> become intimately dependent on His guidance.

November 10

Given to God

"Amaziah asked the man of God, 'But what about the hundred talents I paid for these Israelite troops?' The man of God replied,

'The Lord can give you much more than that.'" (2 Chron. 25:9)

Lord, only You can replace everything we have ever invested in, whether we have invested wisely or foolishly. Even though Amaziah paid about 3.75 tons of silver for "a hundred thousand fighting men from Israel" (v. 6), he listened to the Lord's message from a man of God and in obedience dismissed the troops. Yes, God, what wonderful counsel for us to heed: to do what is right and to acknowledge Your direction and counsel is the way to receive true spiritual riches and eternal gain. Amen.

MEDITATION:
Nothing is lost when it is given to God.

> In His hand are our coins...
> Tokens of our surrender to Him.
> Withholding nothing, they're tossed...
> The glory of God is our gain.
> Freely He gives from all that is His
> Manifold blessings of grace.

November 11

The Burden of Falsehood

"'She has not acknowledged that I was the one who gave her the grain, the new wine and oil, who lavished on her the silver and gold—which they used for Baal.'" (Hos. 2:8)

Father, forgive our presumptuous and arrogant attitudes. Today, may we profess and acknowledge with our own words that everything we are or ever hope to become is by the grace of our Lord. The heavens and earth belong to You, the deep seas and all that is in them. You covered the earth with life. Humankind and every creature on the earth were created by Your wondrous hand. Your hand supplies our food. By grace we are given hope and a future. May we lift Your Name in praise! Amen.

MEDITATION:
Pride carries the burden of falsehood.

> Caught in the hedge of pride…
> Arrogance torn from inside.
> God's grace is at work;
> We take a closer look,
> And know that it is
> God Who gives us the
> Ability to make strides!

November 12

Abundant Life

"'For in him we live and move and have our being.' As some of your own poets have said, 'We are his offspring.'" (Acts 17:28)

You are our lifeblood, O Lord. You give us breath and command the sun to rise, the moon to give us light, and the stars to shine. Your Spirit renews our minds and cleanses our souls. We are precious stones in Your hands, and as we go from glory to glory, it is You Who crowns us with goodness and mercy. We are precious gems—costly was the purchase of our souls. Amen.

MEDITATION:
Abundant life is lived through Christ.

> Life would not make sense
> Without the Lord's recompense.
> Sins remembered no more—
> Enter through the Open Door.

November 13

His Spirit Revives Us

"O Lord, hear my prayer, listen to my cry for mercy; in your faithfulness and righteousness come to my relief." (Ps. 143:1)

You know each one of us by name, and with great mercy You meet us at our point of need. You are very near the brokenhearted.

Stirred with compassion, You embrace us, giving us comfort, blessing us with Your peace. O Lord, with a firm and loving hand, You pick us up and set our feet on solid ground. In Your presence is life forevermore. Amen.

MEDITATION:
Our sovereign Lord hears our cries, and His Spirit revives us.

> Lord, we need You.
> Your eyes search our hearts
> Asking, *"Do you trust Me?"*
> Yes, dear Lord,
> We trust You.
> *"Surrender all to Me."*

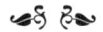

November 14

Love Unwavering

"I will declare that your love stands firm forever, that you established your faithfulness in heaven itself." (Ps. 89:2)

Father, Your love is unwavering. You are a good Father. You are attentive to Your children, ready to listen, eager to hear from us. We have Jesus as our deposit in heaven. Because of His willingness to do Your will and to drink from the cup of wrath, we are spared eternal separation. Your love, Father, reaches to every person. In faithfulness You have made a place for us in heaven. We enter through Jesus. Amen.

MEDITATION:
Love unwavering conquered death.

> Our eyes will close; earthly toil will cease;
> A heavenly home awaits death's defeat.
> Crowns of jewels cast brilliant light…
> Before the throne of eternal life.

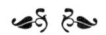

November 15

He is the Shout of Joy

"Worship the Lord with gladness; come before him with joyful songs." (Ps. 100:2)

We worship You, O Lord! Take delight in our praise! You are so very near. We are mesmerized by Your beauty and delight in Your embrace. Holy Spirit, quicken our hearts with "joyful songs," for He is worthy! Open our mouths to sing in prayerful languages, with abandonment, before our King! Amen.

MEDITATION:
He is the shout of joy amidst the din of confusion...the ray of hope shining in darkness.

> Shout! Hosanna!
> Christ is King!
> Savior God is born for thee:
> Incarnate birth lights our way...
> Jesus Christ lives in us today.

ஒ ஓ

November 16

Polished Gems

"You will be a crown of splendor in the Lord's hand, a royal diadem in the hand of your God." (Isa. 62:3)

Father, it is difficult to understand our immeasurable value. In Your hand, we are treasures...royal power radiates through us. We become "a crown of splendor" for our King! From ashes to beauty, O Lord, painstakingly and wondrously, our lives begin to glow like polished jewels. Thank You, for daily working in our lives, chiseling, cutting, and polishing rough, ragged pieces into precious jewels for Christ! Amen.

MEDITATION:
Jagged stones become polished gems.

From jagged stone
To polished gem—
O God, create
A royal diadem!
Remove sin's tarnish
From precious jewels;
Create in Your hand
Lustrous, golden hues.

November 17

First Place

"You shall have no other gods before me." (Exod. 20:3)

When we put "things" before You, Lord, please forgive us. When we are tempted to put ambitions or possessions in first place in our lives, immediately help us, O God, to see the error of our ways. May Your will be done in our lives. Move through us, accomplishing those things Your heart desires. Amen.

MEDITATION:
If God is not first in our lives, another god is.

Come, Lord,
Occupy the space…
Fill my heart…
Take first place.

November 18

Our Undivided Attention

"'But I am the Lord your God, who brought you out of Egypt. You shall acknowledge no God but me, no Savior except me.'"
(Hos. 13:4)

Father, authority and wisdom belong to You. Whatever we put our trust in, we have acknowledged to be our authority. Mistaken authority, in the choosing of other gods, devastates and ruins many lives. Father, forgive us for opening the door to evil influences. May we heed Your admonishment and trust in You. Open our eyes to falsehood…the manipulation of the truth. We confess there is no other God but You. Amen.

MEDITATION:
Intimacy with God requires our undivided attention.

> O Lord, thoughts do roam
> During moments all alone.
> Enemies trespass on mental ground;
> Tiredness seeps in for a round…
> Safeguard my mind from arrest;
> Help me focus on Your loveliness.

ঌ ঌ

November 19

God Responds

"""I spoke to them, but they did not listen; I called to them, but they did not answer.""" (Jer. 35:17b)

Father, forgive us when we choose not to listen. Quickly we run in the opposite direction. Our minds race with our self-interests, certain that we are right. Haven't we foolishly thought our way is superior to Your way? When we sin and refuse Your counsel, anxiety grips our soul and darkens our countenance. We turn to You and seek Your will. In mercy, You cleanse us and reveal our self-righteousness. We look to You. Your healing grace restores us. Amen.

MEDITATION:
God hears and listens and responds…do we?

> We hear the wind softly singing as it whistles
> Through the reddish, golden, sun-glittered leaves…
> Who is the Author of such rapturous melodies?

Colors change as seasons come and go…
The Creator remains the same,
Governing the heavens and earth below.

Do we look at the colorful skies
Thanking God for the golden sunrise?
Or as dusk conceals the sun's rays,
Do we bow before God, Who breathed
Existence into night and day?

Hearing, listening, and responding
Require childlike faith—
A gift of lasting treasure
Overflowing with grace.

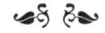

November 20

Christ Makes a Way

"When Jesus saw his mother there, and the disciple whom he loved standing nearby, he said to his mother, 'Dear woman, here is your son,' and to the disciple, 'Here is your mother.' From that time on, this disciple took her into his home." (John 19:26–27)

Dear Jesus, You have placed us in the family of God and given us comfort and love. Amazing love…amazing transformation…amazing healing. All of our needs are met in You. Your perfect love binds our hearts as one. Break our hearts to receive more of You and less of self. Where there is sorrow, You fill us with love. Open our hearts to receive love. Amen.

MEDITATION:
Christ makes a way for us.

Love bore blood for sin;
Man's depravity cut deep within.
Betrayal pierced His blood-soaked side…
With bitter cry we plead,
"O Father, please forgive."

November 21

He is Truth and Life is in Him

"Jesus answered, 'You are right in saying I am a king. In fact for this reason I was born, and for this I came into the world, to testify to the truth. Everyone on the side of truth listens to me.'"
(John 18:37b)

Father, the gospel message of Your saving grace is the truth that sets us free from condemnation. Open ears that are deafened by the world's clamorous ways, touching eyes blinded by sin. You came into this world to save sinners—O Lamb of God, take away the sins that entrap us. Heal our wounded spirits and revive us today. Expose the deceitfulness of our hearts, that we might take hold of Your truth. Amen.

MEDITATION:
He is Truth and life is in Him.

> God's perfect gift is before us. Receive life and
> celebrate His presence. Obedience to God's
> voice, in the message of His Word, is mani-
> fested in our characters and personalities.
> Living out the life of Christ is a testament to
> our faith.

November 22

God's Directives

"Whether you turn to the right or to the left, your ears will hear a voice behind you, saying, 'This is the way; walk in it.'"
(Isa. 30:21)

Our confidence is in the Guardian of our souls, Who orders our steps. We are safe to explore new places, for Your grace and mercy follow us wherever we may go. You are our counsel and wisdom. We are free to make choices, knowing that You are with us. Doors of opportunity will open; other doors will close. Let us not be afraid to go forward with assurance and steadfast trust. Amen.

MEDITATION:
Yielding to God's directives brings steadiness to each step taken.

Frustration mounted.
Bewildered, I cried,
"Which way, Lord?
The way is narrow…
The choices are many."
My Spirit is with you…
Trust and follow Me.
"Now faith is being sure
of what we hope for
and certain of what we do not see" (Heb. 11:1).
God's Word is peace…
We can trust His leading.

November 23

Seek the Face of God

"Let your eyes look straight ahead, fix your gaze directly before you." (Prov. 4:25)

Lord, help us to stay focused, giving us discernment to shut out distractions. Pressing in closer to You, may our ears and hearts become sensitive to Your inner prompting. You are Wisdom. Our hope is in You, Lord. You are our past, present, and future. Your eyes are always on us. May we behold Your gaze! Amen.

MEDITATION:
Look upward and seek the face of God.

God is with us in our daily walk. Although life changes can bring us to a place of sorrow or to a road of recovery, we need not be confounded. Our Redeemer endured our suffering and through Him we will overcome.

※

November 24

Paying Attention to the Little Things

"Above all else, guard your heart, for it is the wellspring of life."
(Prov. 4:23)

Father, You admonish us to guard the very core of our being. We need to hold in check our carnal man. Help us to honor You in thought, word, and deed. Holy Spirit, flow through us and purify our "wellspring of life." We need Your strength to lead us away from temptation. The Christian life can only be lived through You. May You find us sensitive to Your guidance and obedient to Your leading. O Lord, Your Word counsels and protects. It is a shield around us. We prepare for battle as we put on the supernatural armor designed for our use. Your Word is hidden in our heart, O God—a sentry at the door of faith. Amen.

MEDITATION:
Paying attention to the little things that prick our consciences prevents the bigger things from controlling our lives.

> Pain is a symptom of disorder—
> The disturbance of the soul,
> Fighting within our bodies,
> Beyond our own control.
> Bringing attention to our maladies—
> Opening eyes to stark realities,
> We cry out for God's Holy Oil
> To soothe broken hearts
> And heal crushing blows.

※

November 25

The Light of the World

"My eyes are ever on the Lord, for only he will release my feet from the snare." (Ps. 25:15)

Lord, sometimes our struggles are so intense. Help us vow to keep our eyes on You…trusting in Your presence and help. May we commit our ways unto You, for You will direct and order our steps. And during our times and seasons of testing, merciful Lord, please uphold us in the bosom of Your perpetual care. We find in You a dwelling place of hope and renewal and rest. Joy and peace are the covering of Your pavilion. May we lift up our eyes and know our confidence is in You. Amen.

MEDITATION:
May our eyes behold the Light of the world, our Savior.

> To behold His ever-present face is a grace gift from God. Looking into God's face, we begin to embrace the truth about ourselves. We must not be willing to deny or overlook any hidden faults as the Holy Spirit exposes the destructiveness and futility of human pride. For to see Jesus in every day miracles and to have tasted the heavenly Manna, we have already acknowledged God's truth that He has raised a standard of holiness to guard our hearts against evil.

৵ ৽

November 26

Our Actions

"Even a child is known by his actions, by whether his conduct is pure and right." (Prov. 20:11)

We can say all the right things, but our actions are the litmus test. Your Word says, "As water reflects a face, so a man's heart reflects the man" (Prov. 27:19). You know the true character deep inside each one of us. And it isn't very long before our "true colors" are revealed. Help us not to hide from the truth, Lord, but to openly confess our faults and weaknesses as we come to Your throne of grace for pardon. Amen.

MEDITATION:
Our actions set the stage for the true character inside us.

> Unfelt smiles and hidden frowns
> Squelch feelings of despair.
> A heart is breaking—
> Masquerading,
> Fearful to be found.
>
> The Holy Spirit lights the wick,
> Illumining a heart that's sick.
> Taking off the mask of pride,
> He frees the child from inside.

November 27

Christ is our Burden Bearer

"'We must go through many hardships to enter the kingdom of God,' they said." (Acts 14:22b)

Lord, what comfort it is to know that You come along side us and together we "go through many hardships." Safe in Your arms—at peace in Your presence. We can be thankful knowing that hardships purify and prepare us for higher spiritual ground, as we learn empathy, compassion, discernment, understanding, wisdom, and forgiveness. Teach us how to wholeheartedly bring our will in agreement with Your will. Remind us, dear Lord, that we will reach the summit, together. Amen.

MEDITATION:
Hardships are not borne alone when Christ is our Burden Bearer.

Circumstances cannot uproot us;
Strong roots grow deep below.
Winds may blow harshly all around,
But *we are standing on holy ground.*
Borne on eagles' wings of glory,
Our burden bearer lifts our worries.
For Emmanuel—"God" with us—
Is the Savior of our souls.

November 28

In Plain View

"'[Y]our adulteries and lustful neighings, your shameless prostitution! I have seen your detestable acts on the hills and in the fields. Woe to you, O Jerusalem! How long will you be unclean?'"
(Jer. 13:27)

Father, how could we ever escape Your watchful eye? Where would we run? Our lives are laid bare before You. Let us cry out and acknowledge that we need You. May we quickly respond to Your warning, forsaking all idols, making You first in our lives. O God, may we ever be aware of Your love and presence in our lives. For we are Your dwelling place, the temple of the Holy Spirit. Forgive us our sins and heal our bodies and minds from the ravages of sin and the foolishness and darkness of rebellion. Let us receive the hard words with repentant sorrow, allowing Your Spirit to restore us. Amen.

MEDITATION:
God's creation is always in plain view.

Denial has no room to hide,
With God's searchlight
Beaming bright inside.
His powerful Word
Lights the soul's dark night,
Dividing fiction
From truthful plight.

Weighed down by sin,
On bent knee we face,
God's forgiving grace.

◈◈

November 29

Saving Grace

"'Do not be afraid of those who kill the body but cannot kill the soul. Rather, be afraid of the One who can destroy both soul and body in hell.'" (Matt. 10:28)

Grace sets us free from the bondage of sin and death. Grace heals our soul and restores us to wholeness. Grace unlocks the invisible bars of our corruptive captivity. And by grace, Your precious grace, Father, we are saved from damnation and sealed with Your Holy Spirit—forever! We owe our lives to Your grace of salvation. Amen.

MEDITATION:
Freely we have received the benefits of Christ's death, burial, and resurrection. May we freely share His saving grace with others.

Like a river flowing was shed blood—
A testimony of God's love,
As crimson red poured out His side,
Blood-soaked ground opened wide.
Death covered Him with cruel men's scorn;
What was lost was reborn
On the glorious resurrection morn!

◈◈

November 30

Service to God

"It was he who gave some to be apostles, some to be prophets, some to be evangelists, and some to be pastors and teachers, to prepare

God's people for works of service, so that the body of Christ may be built up." (Eph. 4:11–12)

Gracious Lord, purpose and fruition has been granted to us through "works of service" in Your name. Touch our hearts with love that ministers to others, accomplishing Your will, as the Spirit pervades our soul. Take us to the heights of victory and teach purification in the valley of testing. Obedient hearts beat a rhythm of rest and action, fully dependent on and by the summons of God. And together, we march to Christ's processional, as we listen to and obey His voice. Amen.

MEDITATION:
Service to God is in everyday matters of the heart.

God is recognized
By our hearts' overflow,
As "works of service"
And occupations are
Yielded to His control.
Mysteriously He moves,
Gently calling us to Himself...
A flowing current
Of transforming power
Purifying lifeless souls.
O we must learn to trust Him
As we seek our lifelong goals,
For it is God Who orders our steps
And becomes manifested in our souls.
Ah! His nature is taking form,
In the Body of His redeemed;
The reality of Jehovah's presence
Is removing condemnation,
And setting souls free!

December 1

Belief in God's Son

"Jesus said to her, 'I am the resurrection and the life. He who believes in me will live, even though he dies.'" (John 11:25)

By Your flawless Word, Father, we receive comfort to heal our sorrows. Your Word is the anchor of our souls. Grief and disappointment cannot tear our souls out of the palm of Your hand. Connected to You, spirit to Spirit, we are kept safely in Your bosom. And should we succumb to feelings of despair and become weary, we know that our sorrow is being undergirded by the prayers of "a man of sorrows" (Isa. 53:3) Who intercedes for us day and night. Your truth prevails, giving light to a dark situation, as we remember that our risen Savior holds life in His resurrected power. Amen.

MEDITATION:
Belief in God's Son gives us a heavenly position.

> In the canopy of darkness
> Someone seeks freedom
> From evil's relentless quest
> For the soul's consumption.
> Jesus passes by, unveiling His light,
> And spiritual birth is pronounced!

December 2

His Wondrous Manifestations

"When Peter saw this, he said to them: 'Men of Israel, why does this surprise you? Why do you stare at us as if by our own power or godliness we had made this man walk?'" (Acts 3:12)

It is a great but hard thing to perceive, dear Lord—Your mighty power working through us as we witness wondrous manifestations. How profound! A mystery cloaked with indescribable love and wisdom. You create us to shine like the starry hosts in the dark expanse of the skies. Apart from You, we would have no eternal light. May people perceive Your working power in us and the fruit of the Spirit. Keep us connected to You. How can a branch survive or produce fruit if it is severed from the life-giving Vine? O flow through our bodies and nourish our souls that we might glorify Your name. Amen.

MEDITATION:
    We are witnesses and vessels of His wondrous manifestations.

> The glory of God rests upon us…
> All of our days He has ordained.
> Face to face we will stand before Him—
> A servant before a King's questioning gaze!
> God's heavenly treasures are preserved—
> And will be received from the Master's hands.
> Know the splendor of His righteousness—
> Life regenerated and made whole.
> Let us meet the morning with gladness,
> Embrace the light of the soul.
> For in just a little while we will answer
> God's summons into courts of praise!

୶ଽ ଽ୶

December 3

God's Creative Power

"'To whom will you compare me? Or Who is my equal?' says the Holy one." (Isa. 40:25)

Heavenly Father, the firmament beholds the beauty of our Lord as the horizon dazzles in crimson wonder. A spectacular display of Your sovereignty lifts our souls to meet the day as we stand in awe and adoration before You. Thank You, omnipotent Creator! Amen.

MEDITATION:
    God's creative power produces reflecting light in man.

Creation displays God's wondrous power.
Man reflects God's creative power within.

※ ※

December 4

Eternal Value

"Wisdom is supreme; therefore get wisdom. Though it cost all you have, get understanding." (Prov. 4:7)

Lord, a right relationship with You is the wisest thing we could ever seek. There is no greater pursuit or attainment than to cultivate an intimate relationship with You. Teach us this truth, Father, that we might faithfully teach our children and our children's children. For Your teaching is supreme, and life is in the Word. Above all else, help us to guard our hearts from deceptive practices. Amen.

MEDITATION:
On earth we accumulate many things, of which none have eternal value.

> God's wisdom cannot be attained apart from the Word. For the wisdom from above is found in God our Creator. While on earth, we must do those things in which God has purposed and planned. We will be summoned to occupations and vocations where we can use our gifts and talents and skills—all to the glory of God. For the Lord who has created us has given us the ability to reach our maximum potential in Christ. One day our work on earth will cease and our soul's ascension to heaven will be the climax of our earthly life.

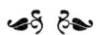

※ ※

December 5

Human Wisdom is Flawed

"Wisdom is a shelter as money is a shelter, but the advantage of knowledge is this: that wisdom preserves the life of its possessor." (Eccl. 7:12)

Eternal Christ our King! Let us taste Your Word and be satisfied with all manner of godliness. For godly wisdom achieves great gain. Without wisdom knowledge is in vain. Your thoughts are higher than our thoughts, O Lord (Isa. 55:8); Who can counsel the Lord? (1 Kings 22:5). From the beginning was Wisdom—O let us ascribe to the wisdom of God. Amen.

MEDITATION:
Human wisdom is flawed in its futile attempt to have knowledge apart from God.

> Earthly limited wisdom,
> Pompous in its regal style,
> Looming over the mind
> It's self-important desires.
> Human wisdom falls short
> Of God's perfect knowledge...
> Lacking His perspective...
> Blinded by no guidance!

▄§ ۊ▄

December 6

His Wondrous Benefits

"Each of you should look not only to your own interests, but also to the interests of others." (Phil. 2:4)

Dear Jesus, without Your intervention, our futile attempts toward mastery over our own lives would prove disastrous. Our lives from beginning to end are in full view of Your spiritual scope. Your thoughts and ways are superior to ours, dear Lord. And as You work and dwell in us, fill us to overflowing with a zealous attitude and give us open hearts to bring pleasure to You. Let our lives demonstrate the distinction between those who know You and those who are estranged from You, that they too will seek Your face. Amen.

MEDITATION:
Praise God for His plan of salvation and all His wondrous benefits.

> How do you explain what is not fully understood?
> Lives changed—opened windows of the soul—
> Where love runs deep and hearts begin to yearn.
> We even do those things we said we could not,
> Speaking wisdom from precepts we have learned.
> Quietly and mysteriously God moves to teach us
> "To will and to act according to his good purpose" (Phil. 2:13).
> Oh this is grace, God's awesome grace!
> Love that Jesus taught us to embrace...
> Providence comes on our journey of faith.

December 7

Lips of Praise

"From the lips of children and infants you have ordained praise because of your enemies, to silence the foe and the avenger."
(Ps. 8:2)

Father, praise silences the enemy and stills the vengeance of man. To ordain praise brings glory and honor to You Who inhabits the praises of Your people. We are filled with Your presence as You occupy our hearts—and we are kept safe from our enemies. No foe can defeat nor thwart Your plans. As it is spoken it is. All-powerful Lord, reign in our hearts today. Amen.

MEDITATION:
Lips of praise sing God's love throughout the earth.

Songs of praise throughout the earth
Celebrate Emmanuel's birth...
Our God is with us.
Lift up a banner of joyous profession...
(Proclaim the grace of salvation)...
Christ reigns in our lives today!
Rejoice! Rejoice! Sweet praises sing...
We're in the audience of a King...
O Christ inhabits our praise!

ஃ ஃ

December 8
God's Respect and Great Love

"But the Lord Almighty will be exalted by his justice, and the holy God will show himself holy by his righteousness. Then sheep will graze as in their own pasture; lambs will feed among the ruins of the rich." (Isa. 5:16–17)

Dear Father, justice and mercy are Your holy scepters. Restoration and revival are a healing balm to our shame. Blessings flow from Your River of peace washing away our debris. Wholeness comes from a relationship with Your Son, Jesus Christ, for the Anointed bore the stripes of our healing. O Lord, may You find delight in Your children as we walk in the ways of Christ, wholly yielded to the standard He has raised according to His Word. Amen.

MEDITATION:
God's respect and great love toward us negate our feelings of shame.

Clothed in royalty,
Resplendent in garments of praise...
Joyously living life through Christ
Who has conquered sorrow and shame.

Filthy rags once worn,
Now cast aside,
Christ has borne our disgrace.

❧ ☙

December 9

Refusal and Failure Go Hand in Hand

"'They refused to listen and failed to remember the miracles you performed among them.'" (Neh. 9:17a)

Father, forgive our stubborn attitudes and pretenses. The air of arrogance becomes a suffocating stronghold when we give in to the falsehood of pride. When we open the door to sin and close the door to belief, we break Your heart. How can we forget the miracles You have performed in our lives? The miracles of rebirth, restoration, and wholeness are present-day miracles. Father, forgive us for our complacency in not seeking the Christ Child and His miraculous rebirth in hearts every day. Let it not be said of Your children, "They refused to listen and failed to remember the miracles You performed among them." Amen.

MEDITATION:
Refusal and failure go hand in hand when we decide to spurn God's counsel.

> Thoughts that are sheathed in deception and opposition to Christ's commands betray our conscience. But by keeping our mind focused on God's Word, we can determine truth from fallacy. The Holy Spirit is our Teacher.

❧ ☙

December 10

His Voice

"[F]or the Lord will be your confidence and will keep your foot from being snared." (Prov. 3:26)

Dear Lord, we turn to You and trust in Your supremacy, being confident in Your providential care. For You will release in us Your strength, might, and wisdom. Help us not to be ensnared by fear, but to walk in the freedom of Christ, knowing that Your presence is a shield around us. Open our ears to hear the gentleness of Your reassuring whisperings as we press in to Your bosom for shelter. And open our eyes to see the stark reality of Your faithfulness, even in the eye of the storm. Amen.

MEDITATION:
His voice cannot be heard above the din of constant chatter, nor can the pride of stubborn hearts welcome His counsel.

> To hear the rhythm of God's heart,
> We must find quiet time apart.

※ ※

December 11

Our Confidence

"Trust in the Lord forever, for the Lord, the Lord, is the Rock eternal." (Isa. 26:4)

Gentle Shepherd, may nothing in this world crowd out our intimacy. In the quiet moments, and in the waiting stations of life, I hear Your voice and know Your presence. Your thoughts become my thoughts as You renew my mind. And I learn how to trust as I allow You to work in my life. Amen.

MEDITATION:
Where our confidence is placed will be our trust.

> Heavenly dew saturates the earth…
> God's mercy, rich and sweet.
> His trustworthiness satisfies
> And we are refreshed again.

※ ※

December 12

Haughtiness

"The pride of your heart has deceived you." (Obad. 3a)

Father, we can boast only in You. All that we have has come from Your mighty hand; "But remember the Lord your God, for it is he who gives you the ability to produce wealth" (Deut. 8:18a). Thank You, Lord, for richly supplying our needs and prospering our souls. Keep us from the destructive downfall of pride. Like a domino effect, deception will knock down everything we attempt to construct from the pride of our hearts. Give us Your perspective on the issues of the heart and allow no vainglory in our hearts. Amen.

MEDITATION:
Haughtiness dims the eyes of the soul.

> Every blessing is from above. Victory and success come from God's favor. God uses many people to help shape our lives and give life to our dreams. He interweaves many circumstances in the tapestries of our lives to complete the bigger picture. When we live life His way, recognizing His hand upon our shoulders, we will rejoice in Christ who orders our steps.

December 13

Held Together

"In his hand is the life of every creature and the breath of all mankind." (Job 12:10)

Lord, all wisdom, power, and knowledge belong to You. You hold the world. In a moment, at the command of Your voice, You can summon us into Your eternal presence. We bless and honor Your holy name. Nothing goes unnoticed before Your searching eyes. Always You are with us; always You are faithful. Give us rest in pleasant places, strengthen us in the battle marches, and deliver us from the tyranny of our enemies. Amen.

MEDITATION:
   He is preeminent in beauty and love, and we are held together.

> Loveliness adorns His nature…
> Purest gold perfected and tried.
> Garments drenched in fragrant holiness…
> Apparel fashioned by Almighty God.
> Voices proclaim praises and devotion;
> Untold millions kneel before their King…
> Anthems sweet cry out the renderings
> From thankful hearts bowed at His feet.

December 14

Unquenchable Love

"May the peoples praise you, O God; may all the peoples praise you." (Ps. 67:5)

How wonderful are Your ways, O God. Lord, we give thanks for life and all our provisions and the blessings and tests that give us strength. Guard our hearts against any resistance to Your plan, purpose, and direction for our lives. Merciful and gracious are You, O Lord. Fresh insights and understanding are given to us, and we are forever changed. Praise and honor are sung from the tablets of our hearts and the fruit of our lips, for our hearts beat with Your love flowing through us. Amen.

MEDITATION:
   God's gifts to us are good: unquenchable love reflects His radiance and goodness.

> God's goodness is manifested in our hearts…
> Gentleness and mercy stir within.

Unfolding drama takes center stage…
The Master directs the script.
And, once again, Love delights our senses…
We are to forgive and are forgiven.
God purges the soul…
He is in control.
Our God is beautiful…
Supremacy and majesty adorn Him.
He invades our thoughts with His thoughts,
And we are forever changed…
Free to follow Him.

❧ ☙

December 15
God's Ways

"Since they did not know the righteousness that comes from God and sought to establish their own, they did not submit to God's righteousness." (Rom. 10:3)

Father, I pray that we will know and submit to Your moral and just ways. There is a built-in protection for those who believe and allow You to be their guide. When we make good choices based upon Your Word, and not according to the world's written or spoken code, we have all Your promises as our wondrous assurance. Father, keep us in the sweet intimacy of fellowship with Your Son Jesus. And for those that do not know You, reveal to them the destructive paths they travel. Soften hearts to trust and accept You in their lives. In Jesus' name. Amen.

MEDITATION:
God's ways were created to protect and guide and bless us along our earthly journeys.

Tensions rise from misguided ways…
Dressed in foolish pride…
Truth stares from every corner…
Painful lessons wear sorrowful expressions…
And running ahead can really slow you down.

God's heart weeps as we struggle to learn…
Patiently he waits for our return.
Eagerly He sweeps us up into His arms,
Providing forgiveness and healing balm.

Sojourning on God's guided path—
On a journey that only He can bless—
Through Christ we complete
The mission He has asked.

ഛ ഇ

December 16

A Mind Fit for Battle

"Be on your guard; stand firm in the faith; be men of courage; be strong." (1 Cor. 16:13)

Lord, thank You for Your written and spoken Word, which alerts us to our enemy's desire to devour us. Your provisions have given us safety, boldness, and strength. For it is by Your power and wisdom and grace that we have been given daily direction and counsel. You provide a way through the struggles. We are encouraged by those who have gone before us. They become our mentors—hope in the midst of struggles. Help us to be truly Your disciples and to follow You, empowering us to finish the race. Amen.

MEDITATION:

A mind firmly placed on Christ is a mind fit for battle.

Roaming thoughts find no solace
Where seeds of despair are sown.
Defeat springs up to greet the 'morn,
Casting shadows upon unripe souls.

Cut down like plants that danced then bled—
Frail bodies pummeled in evil's stead
With dashed hopes void of His still peace—
We sing: O come to us, blessed King!

Whispered prayers ascended to His throne
And power flowed into our very souls
As our thoughts remained fixed on Him.
"Arise!" He whispered in our ear,
"Be bold and do not fear...
Ushered into rest are saints above
Who have trusted their lives
To My great love...
Be still, and know that I am God" (Ps. 46:10).

December 17

The Frailty of Humankind

"The Lord is slow to anger and great in power; the Lord will not leave the guilty unpunished." (Nah. 1:3a)

Dear Lord, we do not escape Your correction. It is because You love us that we are disciplined. We are thankful You are a God of justice and mercy. Convict us of our sinful ways so that we may turn from evil and do what is good. Grant us the heart of a servant: a contrite spirit and a willing heart to listen and follow Your voice. Shape our attitudes according to the nature of Your precious Son. And when the scalpel begins to do surgery on our hearts, uphold us with Your mighty hand of mercy, lest our bones dry within and we cry out, "O Lord, heal me, for my bones are in agony" (Ps. 6:2b). Restore us to Your joyful presence, for "All the days of the oppressed are wretched, but the cheerful heart has a continual feast" (Prov. 15:15). Amen.

MEDITATION:
Justice and mercy embrace the frailty of humankind.

God's justice and mercy,
Dispensed according to His great love,
Give correction leading to repentance.
A loving Father leads by example:
Christ is the perfect image of God.

Though we are frail, He is our Strength.
He Who knows our innermost feelings and thoughts
Desires to transform our hearts into godly chambers
Of holiness and confidence,
That we might follow His lead
With the quiet assurance of a soul
Stirred by His justice and mercy.

∽§ ३∾

December 18
Recognizable by the Spirit's Revelation

"The Lord your God is with you, he is mighty to save."
(Zeph. 3:17a)

Voices echo through our minds. Fleeting thoughts dart about creating mental pictures. We are bombarded with worldly stimuli. Help us sort out the conflicting messages. Ring morality and justice and compassion in our ears. You are our encouragement and hope… "mighty to save"! We are filled with Your Spirit and sustained by Your prayers. You live to intercede for us, and through Your glorious intervention we are saved. Tenderly You call; tenderly You come. O Lamb of God, come. Amen.

MEDITATION:
Unrecognizable by the naked eye, but recognizable by the Spirit's revelation—our inner witness that our Lord is with us.

Fear invades our bodies…
Wrestling against the soul.
Warfare rages…
On the battlefield of our mind.
Light breaks through the struggle…
God's word comes alive.
Armor bearers are we,
Who take our stand,

Believing victory is close at hand.

December 19

Planted in Our Hearts, Watered by Faith

"I have brought you glory on earth by completing the work you gave me to do." (John 17:4)

Lord, we bring You pleasure whenever we step out in faith, trusting Your direction and relying on Your empowerment to complete the work You gave us to do. Keep us on the track of obedience, sensitive to Your desires, eager to bring You glory. Amen.

MEDITATION:
God's seed planted in our hearts, watered by faith, is perfected by His love.

> Stepping out in faith,
> Secure in Your arms,
> I sense Your presence,
> Love's sweet fragrance.
> Your desires become
> Desires of my own…
> Dying to self,
> I am free to follow
> My Love on earth,
> "Completing the work
> You gave me to do."

December 20

Grace Leads

"It is because of him that you are in Christ Jesus, who has become for us wisdom from God—that is, our righteousness, holiness, and redemption." (1 Cor. 1:30)

Lord, let us become light in the path of a seeker's heart—bold believers who trust and obey the Spirit's prompting. Today, may those who are downcast discover the hope and reality of Christ Jesus. Break down the barriers of fear, poverty, or hatred—strongholds that can prevent ears that hear (Matt. 11:15). And grant us the grace to show compassion to those in need. Amen.

MEDITATION:
Grace leads us to everlasting life.

What do you see?
Vanity chases the wind.
Share Christ.
Give hope.

December 21

The Mind of Christ

"Do not be wise in your own eyes; fear the Lord and shun evil."
(Prov. 3:7)

Father, give us wisdom. Help us to be aware of man's wisdom and its deception. Draw us closer to You and further away from the world and its vain and empty philosophies. May we be esteemed by You and not by man. Amen.

MEDITATION:
The mind of Christ is nurtured and fed by His word.

I call you by name.
Will you come?
There's much work that needs to be done.
Take no tools, only receive what I give.
Enter the Kingdom of My glorified Son.
Wisdom from on high will clothe you.
Every need will be met in Jesus' name.
Follow the footprints of a King.

Read His word and learn from Him.

December 22

Invisible Bars

"Set me free from my prison, that I may praise your name." (Ps. 142:7a)

Heavenly Father, we all experience seasons of heart-wrenching pain. We are comforted knowing You are with us in our pain. It is during these moments—for next to eternity these are moments—that we are being spiritually stretched as we learn to exercise patience, love, and trust. In the darkness reveal to us the truth. "The path of the righteous is like the first gleam of dawn, shining ever brighter till the full light of day" (Prov. 4:18). As we turn to You, dear Father, for counsel and wisdom, teach us how to make every day count for Your name's sake. For it is in the tight, hemmed-in compartments we remain still long enough to hear Your voice. Speak to us, Father. Set us free. Amen.

MEDITATION:
Invisible bars can imprison us. Jesus delivers us from all our fears.

Show me the upward path…
Stilled in my sorrow and pain,
With bowed knees I humbly ask:
"Set me free from my prison,
That I may praise Your name."

December 23

Enveloped in His Power

"Then the Spirit of God came upon Zechariah son of Jehoiada the priest." (2 Chron. 24:20a)

You clothe us with Your Spirit. O God, our future is built on the Rock Who is strong and eternal. Grant us the courage to make a difference in our workplaces and other areas of influence, for we are a testament to and a witness of Your amazing grace that has transformed us into children of God. Amen.

MEDITATION:
Enveloped in His power and consecrated by His grace.

He watches over us...
O saints, tarry on!
God never grows weary;
Lacking nothing He presses on.

The Spirit of God is with us,
Arranging circumstance...
Faith is an adventure...
Our feet will cross another's path.

Divine appointments
To encourage hearts,
To dry tears from eyes...
Good News to weary travelers
Who need God's healing balm

ఆర్ ఏ

December 24

When the Lord has First Place

"Bitterly she weeps at night, tears are upon her cheeks. Among all her lovers there is none to comfort her" (Lam. 1:2)

Father, only You can meet all our needs. Your love satisfies our hungry souls. You have created us and know us intimately. What belongs to You, let no man divide. We are Your people and You are our God. If left on our own, our souls would perish. But, You have sealed us with Your Spirit. And one day we will see You face-to-face. Your greatness, O God, overshadows us with indescribable love. Amen.

MEDITATION:
When the Lord has first place in our lives, our lives will reflect His glory.

> Crowned with God's mercy,
> We lift our voices and sing...
> Wearing the helmet of salvation,
> We give praise to our King.
> No need to fret or worry;
> God is watching faithfully.
> He is our Lord...
> He hears our every plea.

ઇઙ ૩૭

December 25

God's Armor of Faith

"He replied, 'You of little faith, Why are you so afraid?'"
(Matt. 8:26a)

Lord, our faith is small because our knowledge of Your power is small. Come, Lord Jesus, and increase our understanding; open our minds to the knowledge of Your wondrous name. Your grace is sufficient to bring us safely through every storm. Grant us the courage to step out and to meet You in the howling winds and in the blast furnace. In loving faithfulness, You are always with us, teaching spiritual truths. With loving kindness, You are preparing us for greater works. Gently You lead. Your shield is about us. Amen.

MEDITATION:
Fear's paralyzing sting is no match for God's armor of faith.

> To know God is to trust Him
> Through life's perilous ways...
> For it is in the heat of the furnace
> And in the stark cold of the darkness

That we discover the Lord is with us.

December 26

Belief

"'Do you believe that I am able to do this?' 'Yes, Lord,' they replied." (Matt. 9:28b)

Dear Lord, please forgive my unbelief. It is just as You say—now help me take You at Your Word. There are signs and miracles all around us. One look at the heavens and we see Your design amongst the stars in the universe. At Your command, the sun appears over the horizon and sets at the prescribed time of day. You hold everything together in perfect balance. Why, Lord, do I fail to grasp Your power? Lord, help me to take hold of Your truths and apply them to my mind. For "Your word is a lamp to my feet and a light for my path" (Ps. 119:105). Amen.

MEDITATION:
Belief is supported by action.

> Unbelief has its own suffering,
> Entangled in hopelessness…
> What a pity to be so near to Jesus
> And not recognize the Truth.

December 27

A Great Return

"'I tell you the truth, unless a kernel of wheat falls to the ground and dies, it remains only a single seed. But if it dies, it produces many seeds.'" (John 12:24)

Father, as we trust our lives into Your hands, dying to self—giving up the old nature for Your nature—multiply our faith. Direct our footsteps and strengthen our hearts. Give us assignments that will glorify Your name. Create in us the desire to reach our God-given potential as we seek to accomplish Your perfect will through the tasks given us. And when the labor is hard, remind us to "Come to [You]" (Matt. 11:28), where we will find rest for our souls. Amen.

MEDITATION:
Seed that is sown and pulverized in the earth yields a great return as it matures.

> Letting go of "our way"
> And taking hold of "His way"
> Is a walk of trust…
> We walk by faith.
> Placing our hand in His,
> Allowing His lead,
> We discover He is able
> To do all things…
> If only we believe.

December 28

Eternally Changed for His Glory

"[Y]ou will be called by a new name that the mouth of the Lord will bestow." (Isa. 62:2b)

Lord, we are thankful for Your indwelling Spirit creating new life inside us. Change our crusty exteriors into cheerful countenances that radiate trust and joy in our King. Restorative work begins on the inside. Layers upon layers of invalid messages have been recorded on our brains—messages that undermine our faith.

Father, protect our minds from the onslaught of harmful stimuli. Although we live in the world, we must be dressed for spiritual warfare, prepared to "take up the shield of faith" (Eph. 6:16a) and wield Your Word, "the sword of the Spirit" (v. 17a). Help us to stand in Your strength. You've created in us a new name, O Lord. We are the righteousness of Christ. Find delight in Your people; for You are our God. Amen.

MEDITATION:
We are eternally changed for His glory.

> Only God can take the seed of a rose
> And grow it into a beautiful blossom
> Whose fragrance delights the senses.
> Just as unique as the rose
> Is God's transforming touch.
> Pruning time has come…
> Snipping here and there,
> Our Master Gardener cuts,
> And a stronger plant emerges.
> The transformation is worth the struggle.

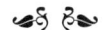

December 29

The Rock of Our Salvation

"[B]uilt on the foundation of the apostles and prophets, with Christ Jesus himself as the chief cornerstone." (Eph. 2:20)

Surround us with Your presence, O Lord. Many faithful witnesses have gone before us. As we walk with You, hand in hand, may You find us faithful. May our testimonies be living stones, "built on the foundation of the apostles and prophets, with Christ Jesus himself as the chief cornerstone"—a witness of our assurance in You. Amen.

MEDITATION:
Jesus Christ is *the Rock of our Salvation*.

> Come, sweet Lord of splendor,
> Radiate love through us.
> Sparkling in obscure, dark corners…
> Living stones of grace and love.

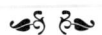

December 30

God is Able

"'Do not be fainthearted or afraid; do not be terrified or give way to panic before them.'" (Deut. 20:3b)

Our hearts are enlarged and encouraged by Your counsel, O God. When You invite us to follow You, You also make the way possible. Settle our hearts, lest we faint. Strengthen our minds, lest we run ahead. Your unconditional love perfects us. Rule our hearts and minds with Your peace. Satisfy our souls with Your righteousness, covering us, O God, with salvation. Amen.

MEDITATION:
God is able.

> God is able…
> Don't say, "I can't," but that "I can."
> What evil has opposed His law?
> Be bold and strong…
> Face fear with courage…
> Faith marches on!

December 31

The Counsel of Christ

"Yet I am always with you; you hold me by my right hand. You guide me with your counsel, and afterward you will take me into glory." (Ps. 73:23–24)

Lord Jesus, the mark of a Christian is love. Because we are growing in Your love, we are in the process of becoming Christlike. Help us to walk in love and to find joy in the journey. We are ambassadors reflecting Your character and attributes. Lord, may we be found faithful in service. Amen.

MEDITATION:
Love means walking in the counsel of Christ.

Lord, walk with me;
I need Your touch…
Rise from Your throne.

Meet needy cries;
I need Your help…
Rise from Your throne.

Visit aching hearts;
I need Your wisdom…
Rise from Your throne.

You've answered cries,
You've touched souls…
Your love has risen in me.

Meditations of the Heart
A Prayer Devotional

can be ordered by sending $8.99
plus $4.00 shipping and handling to:

Joanne L. Gunning
P.O. Box 151674
Cape Coral, FL 33915